MASK OFF

DARYL CLEMES

Print ISBN: 978-1-09832-639-5

eBook ISBN: 978-1-09832-640-1

TABLE OF CONTENTS

INTRODUCTION

This book is about a King, a kingdom, and a royal family. The King is none other than God, the One who created the universe by Himself. The kingdom is His domain, which is technically everywhere. It is very tangible in heaven while it cannot be perceived on earth with the naked eye. The royal family are also the citizens of this kingdom. They have the privilege of professing allegiance to the King while also being related to Him. The members of this royal family have also placed all of their faith in the King, in part, by rejecting all other kingdoms. The people have inherited many benefits and freedoms, prompting them to give thanks and rejoice every day.

Did you know that the gospel is not being taught or preached properly by people and churches? That is not to say that the teaching is incorrect. But, it is incomplete. In fact, Jesus taught the gospel much differently than most people do now-a-days. To understand what Jesus was preaching, we first have to start from the beginning, Genesis. From this book, the entirety of the gospel can be seen. This includes the kingdom of God which was Jesus' main focus during His ministry.

You might know that praying is a good thing to do. Even non-Christians believe this to some degree. But you might not know how and why it works. You see, prayer is not supposed to be a religious activity. Prayer is not supposed to be a series of wishes. Prayer is not supposed to be begging or groveling. Praying is not supposed to be saying the same thing over and over again. Believing wrongly about prayer will cause it to be ineffective. And talking to someone who is not there is hard to wrap our minds around. But there is a practicality to prayer that we will discuss.

The Bible is not a history book. The history in it has been proven or, at least, not unproven time and time again. But history is not the Bible's main focus. Its main focus is to tell the story of a King, His kingdom, and His royal family. The Bible is not a book of advice. It is not just a source of information to be weighed evenly with other sources. The Bible is 100% trustworthy and is right even when we don't understand or agree with it. The people of God know this already but for those who are new to this kind of stuff, proof may be necessary.

Who is God? How does God, Jesus, and the Holy Spirit relate to each other? How does salvation work? What does a man dying on a cross have to do with me? Who is Jesus? The answer to these questions may seem elementary to some. But to those people, let me ask you this: "If you know the answer to these questions so well then why is it that you cannot explain them very well to anyone who asks?" Maybe you need to understand better. Maybe you need to understand differently. We will look at the answer to these questions from a non-religious perspective. All you have to do is open your mind.

Did you know that the church that is seen today does not resemble the one that was seen in Bible times, the first century? It's true! So what happened? When did it change? Is going to church good or bad? Is it even necessary? The world is still very interested in Jesus, to some extent, but has lost all interest in church! We will talk about it.

What does God want you to do? What is your purpose and destiny? These are very important questions to answer. Most people have no clue! Everyone has been put on the earth to do something specifically designed for them. We will discover how to find out what that is for your life.

Mask Off:

I know the title of this book, "Mask Off," does not seem to be related to the subject matter. It will as soon as I can explain some things. But first, I need to define what the title means. We all know that a mask is a covering for the face. Some people wear masks due to respiratory issues. However, almost every other time a mask is worn to conceal or hide something from view, as in a disguise or veil. A mask is used as a manner of expression that hides one's true character or feelings. It is how one attempts to make something that is not the case appear true.

The make-up that women put on is often called a mask. Regardless of the specific reason that one uses it, make-up is intended to cover up what lies beneath. Think about the face of a clown. That person is completely unrecognizable with the make-up. Hollywood uses make-up all the time. Have you ever seen a celebrity photograph without make-up? Old actors look old, blemishes and freckles are seen, and true skin tone is revealed.

We have all seen movies and the nightly news showing bank robbers. They wear masks most of the time. They obviously do not want people to know who they truly are so they put on a fake identity. When they are finally brought to justice, we can see their face on the mugshot. No more hiding for them!

One of my favorite movies is The Mask, starring Jim Carrey. He plays Stanley Ipkiss who finds a magical mask. While wearing the mask, he becomes a supernatural playboy who is charming and confident, the opposite of Stanley's real characteristics. However, Stanley's alter ego also causes some damage. Stanley decides by the end of the movie to throw away the mask and be happy with his true self.

Now that we know what a mask is used for, let me tell you what the purpose of this book is: to remove the facade of religion and tradition in order to reveal the true reality that lies just underneath. The truth is hidden in plain sight. It has been lost in transmission. It has been covered with a veil. Its origins have long been forgotten. The truth is now a mystery but it will be revealed again soon.

Study Guidelines:

There are a few things to remember before you start reading this book:

- The New Living Translation is quoted throughout this book. If another translation is used then there will be a notation afterwards. If there is not a notation then you know that it is a NLT quote.

- I do not quote all scriptures that I reference. I will always note where the Bible passage is found but I may or may not type it out for you. Or I might only type it out partially, leaving the rest for you to find and read.

- Individual study while reading this book is suggested and expected! This book will be a waste of time if you do not want to read the Bible for yourself. I am not God! Do not take my word for stuff. Do not disagree with me without letting the scriptures speak for themselves. If you think you already know something, read it again! I will give prompts throughout this book when to study something. It will be no more than a chapter or two and sometimes less than that. I believe in the Bible read in context but I cannot quote full chapters for you. So sometimes I will prompt you to read something in context rather than just read the one quote that I reference. I want an opportunity to lead you on a journey but you have to walk for yourself. If you do not have a Bible, get one! The Salvation Army, and various other ministries give them away for free. You can also download a Bible app onto your smart phone, computer, tablet, or iPad for free.

- This book has been written from a non-religious and "non-churchy" perspective. Many people will appreciate that. Many people will not. I approach the subject matter differently than you may have heard before. Whether you are new to these subjects or trained, a different perspective will benefit you.

Discovery can only happen after a search has taken place. A cover conceals something. Discovery seeks to reverse that process. That is what Mask Off is all about.

A PERSONAL JOURNEY

My Mom:

Mattie Jean was raised on a farm in Tennessee with two sisters and one brother. Her mother, also named Mattie, was a home maker and a God fearing woman. Her father, Gene, was a chef, a farmer, and a bootlegger. Gene always made sure the kids went to church though. He would often pick up other kids in the neighborhood and take them too. Gene bought a lot of land with the bootlegging money. The church would often hold their tent revivals on one of those large plots. My mother was told that joining a church was the only way to know the Lord. For some reason, she never believed that. Mattie Jean watched people go to the front of the church to accept Jesus as their Lord. Back then, the church would tell people to tarry in order to get saved. Tarrying is when people repeat over and over, "Jesus, Jesus, Jesus" until they have some sort of emotional response.

This might be shaking, crying, shouting, rolling around on the floor, or anything else that is loud.

Mattie Jean would look at all of this from her pew, thinking those people were nuts! She would attend summer Bible camps and even did some secretary work for the church. Yet, the Christian experience was never very real for her. Many years later, Mattie Jean became pregnant with her first child. She was ashamed of herself and felt like she was being judged by everyone. She had a friend in Chicago, Illinois that she could stay with until she got on her feet so, in 1962 Mattie Jean ran away to a big city where she could vanish. No one else knew her there which is the way she wanted it. Mattie Jean thought she was a bad girl and not very valuable after giving her first child away for adoption. So, she began to live a wild lifestyle. This included getting drunk, getting high, partying, and sleeping around.

Mattie Jean made acquaintances with many people over a season of partying in the Chicago club scene on the weekends. However, around 1970, she formed a relationship with one in particular. They had a tumultuous relationship but it lasted for quite a while. In 1977 Mattie Jean became pregnant again and I was born in July of 1978.

One day, Mattie Jean was getting high, listening to music, and watching television with the sound turned down. All of a sudden, out of nowhere, a thought came into her mind that she had never thought of or even considered before. She thought to herself: "Either someone is serving God or they are serving the devil! If you are not serving God then you have no choice but to be serving the devil!" Mattie Jean was astonished at this thought but did not know if it was true or not. So she called her sister, Gloria, back in Tennessee to try and find some answers. She asked Gloria, "Is it true that if you are not serving God then you are serving the devil?" Gloria replied, "Yes." The conversation pretty much ended there. Back then, long distance rates were high and something to be avoided. However, after about three days, Gloria realized that Mattie Jean must have been asking her that question because she was ready to turn her life over to Jesus so, Gloria called Mattie Jean back and apologized for ending the conversation so soon.

Gloria told Mattie Jean very plainly, "God knows that you drink, and smoke, and party, and lay with a man that you are not married to but, God wants you to come as you are today. Most people try and get their life straightened out before they come to Jesus. That does not work. Jesus has to change you Himself." Mattie Jean listened intently while Gloria continued, "Is there anything stopping you from giving your life over to the Lord today?" "No," said Mattie Jean. "Do you believe Jesus died for your sins and then was resurrected on the third day?" Gloria asked. "Yes" said Mattie. "Then that is basically all there is to it" Gloria said. Mattie Jean's sister led her in a prayer that very night.

After that, Mattie Jean began to change on the inside. Whenever she found the time, she would read the Bible. Something that she wanted nothing to do with all of a sudden became totally irresistible, amazing, and fascinating to her. She would even read the Bible while she was getting high. Imagine that! Around that time, in March of 1979, Mattie Jean took her son and moved back home, to Tennessee.

To Train a Child:

The Sunday church service was getting ready to come to a close. But first the pastor needed to give an altar call, a summons to those wishing to show their commitment to Jesus and be saved. At that point in every service, the children's church would let out and flood into the sanctuary. While people were giving their lives to Jesus up front, the parents could gather their kids and prepare for an exit. On this particular morning, Mattie Jean could not find her son. She asked around to see if anyone knew where I was until someone found me. She could not find me because, instead of going where all the other kids were going, I answered the pastor's altar call! I was in the line of people in front of the church waiting to be prayed for and accept Jesus into my life. I was towards the end of my toddler years and entering into my middle childhood years.

Around 1982, my mother was able to find a good enough job to purchase a house. She really couldn't afford it, but it was either raise me in the suburbs or in the inner city projects.

Mattie Jean refused to do that despite recommendations from officials. It was a little 900 square foot house, newly constructed, in a rapidly growing part of town. She even let me pick out the color. I chose yellow and we soon moved in.

My mother and I would talk about everything and she didn't hold any punches regardless of my age. I remember her telling me that nobody is perfect, not even her. I actually got into an argument with some kids in the first grade who thought that parents are perfect. So we took it to the teacher who actually sided with the other kids, agreeing with them that parents are perfect! I still didn't believe it because of what Mattie Jean had told me.

I remember seeing a 100 dollar bill in my mother's hand one day. I thought we were rich! She quickly shut me down. She said "Daryl, any time you see me with a lot of money in my hand like this, it is because I am paying bills. The money is not mine. It is the utility department's. You need to go to school and study. Don't be like me!" I remember Christmas times. My mother never bothered to tell me lies about Santa Claus. During Christmas, she would tell me to write down my Christmas list. Then we would look over it together and pray about it. I always knew that my mom was buying the toys, along with other family. I also knew that I would not be able to receive everything that I wanted. But, I trusted God and my mom! She also told me that the tooth fairy and Easter bunny were both lies. However, I was instructed never to tell the kids at school. She said, "Their parents want them to believe that. That is their business."

I believed in the Lord wholeheartedly very early on. I remember telling a convenience store clerk once that I had just come from the dentist. He wondered out loud how I had the courage to do that. I remember looking at my mom and asking her, "Does he not know?" Then I looked at him and pointed up to the sky. Mattie Jean told me that one weekend when I was sick, she woke up and saw me pacing back and forth with the Bible in my hand praying to God. I would also minister to the kids in my neighborhood. I didn't know I was ministering at the time. I was just being myself. I played children's Christian music outside and invited kids to church.

My mother and I would kneel down and pray before I would go to bed at night. I would pray and she would pray. We read Bible stories from a children's story book and she would answer any questions that I would have. One night, as I lay in bed, I saw a big shadowy fist hovering right above me. Frightened, I called my mother. She prayed and rebuked the spirit in the room. After that, she started playing children Christian music in my room to help me stay calm. Whenever I would see that shadowy fist, I would pray and rebuke it.

I saw several miracles while growing up. These observances played a major part in who I am today. You might not know that many people have one arm or one leg shorter than the other. This can cause physical ailments. Well, one summer at a church camp, I saw arms and legs being grown out with prayer. I tried to get them to pray for me but my arms and legs were even length. One night I was shooting basketball in my driveway when I saw an angel. Another time during Christmas, my mom let me open up an early gift. It was a toy cap gun that transformed into a robot. Somehow I busted the toy. Mattie Jean said we could try and get another one. The next day when I woke up, the toy was fixed. Assuming my mom bought it from a store that morning, I looked outside. There was snow on the ground with no tire tracks. I went and asked her if she had left but she said no. And yet another time, I saw visions in the carpet. The visions I saw were faces. Just like you can see a foot print in plush carpet, I saw the carpet impressed in places that would create the picture of a face and then it would turn into another face.

This story is not obviously a miracle. But one night I had a basketball game to play at the YMCA. However, the driver side door of our car would not stay closed. I nagged and begged her to take me so she figured out a way to tie the door closed with string. We started driving out of our neighborhood when, suddenly, my door came flying open! I tried to close it but it would not stay closed. That ended that and we went back home. I was calm though. I just assumed that God made my door fly open to keep us from leaving that night. I never questioned it.

I don't ever remember my mother and I having conversations about church. When she would speak to me about the

Lord or the Bible, it was without the context of the church. Our conversations about the Lord or the Bible were in the mist of real life situations. I was not raised in a religious household. In fact, she always used to tell me this: "Listening to a preacher is like eating fish. You have to spit out the bones." I even remember when Jimmy Swaggart, an American evangelist, fell from grace after being caught red handed with a prostitute back in 1988. Christians everywhere were so angry. "What a hypocrite" they cried. But my mother wasn't mad. She told me he is just a man. He is not Jesus. And he can be forgiven of his sins. He wasn't put off the air immediately after that and she kept watching him.

Mask On:

My mother and I stopped going to church consistently during my adolescent years. Mattie Jean worked a lot and was often tired. She started sleeping in more and more on Sundays as the years went by. Eventually our attendance whittled down to just going to church once in a while. It was not good for me, a boy in puberty, to be without any church influence.

During this time, my social status at school became a big deal to me. I wanted to be popular. Looking back at it now, I just wanted to be loved and respected. But as we all have done, I went looking for love in all the wrong places and I went about things in completely the wrong way. It's hard to break into another social level at school without having something to offer like parental social status (prestige), athleticism (sports), great looks (attractiveness), or any other type of charisma.

As my school became a little bit more diverse, I met more and more African Americans like myself. I soon realized that if I could hang around them and start acting, "black" (whatever that means), then I could be included in a clique of people that had power and respect in the school. So that is what I did. I began to choose hairstyles like flat tops and afros. I had my ears pierced. And then I actually had to teach myself how to cuss like the rest of the boys! It felt weird at first but it got easier and easier. I changed the way I dressed and the kind of music I listened to. The CDs I began to buy almost all had "parental advisory" labels on them. I also began to walk around with a frown or scowl on my face like many gangster rappers did at the time. Back in the 90s, many African American boys wanted to be "hard" or tough. So that look on my face was like a warning to all bystanders, much like how a rattle snake shakes his tail. Most of my old friends saw me less and less. I was a new man and it wasn't good.

In my early adulthood, I dabbled in many sinful things as most of us have done. Just to name a few, I participated in sex, drunkenness, drugs, and more. Throughout these low times, though, I never stopped believing in God and Jesus. But, I was in a state of rebellion. Rebellion is the action or process of resisting authority or control. I can't say that I had a high level of conviction in my heart during this time, but I knew that how

I was living was wrong and not pleasing to God. I had decided to do things my own way. It wasn't working very well but I was all in. Meanwhile, I kind of always knew that God had a plan for my life. I thought His plan for me had something to do with me acquiring what I had always wanted: money, power, and respect. I also thought that, one day, God would run me down and basically say to me, "No more rebellion! It is time for you to live for me now." I decided that if the Lord ever chose to offer me this proposition that I would take Him up on that offer, no questions asked.

Mask Off:

Fast forward…My wife, Felicia, had been wanting to go to church for some years but I was not interested. I remember one year she dragged me into a New Year's Eve church service. I only went to appease her. I barely remember anything about that service except being glad when it was over. I later expressed to her that I was not interested in church. However, I did not mind going to a Bible study. The problem with that is it is hard to find a Bible study anywhere that is not connected or affiliated with a church.

In 2005, Felicia informed me that her Aunt Belinda had decided to start holding Bible studies from her apartment. She called it, "The Class of Christ." I was not jumping with joy or anything, but I agreed to attend. While attending these courses, for the first time, I was reading the Bible! I had always believed that the Bible was trustworthy but I hardly ever read it though. I guess I just never believed I could understand it but now I was in a Bible class that was completely detached from any church. That made the course appealing. It was all about what the Bible had to say and I was intrigued.

Sometimes the classes would stop being held for a period of time. But Felicia and I would beg Belinda to give us private lessons. She did and we would read the Bible with her. Sometimes Belinda made statements about something the Bible said. But Felicia and I would make her find the passage in the Bible and show us verbatim in black and white. This was before google and smart phones so if Belinda could not remember then she had to comb through her concordance and painstakingly track down the passage.

Despite my increase knowledge of the scriptures, I still had not given my life over to Christ. And I still was not interested in going to a church. But, one Sunday afternoon, Felicia decided that she wanted to go to church. Out of nowhere, she approached me with this desire. It was my first Sunday off work in a long time and I had just climbed into my recliner chair to watch some football. It did not take long for me to give her my answer: "No." Normally Felicia would not go if I was not going but this time was different. She simply said, "Okay," and took the kids with her. She didn't even get mad about it, which was great for me. I was astounded that she did not get angry about not getting her way, and that she left to go without me and, even took the kids with her! When she returned from service, she was in a good mood too! She could not stop talking about the pastor's message. She even read all the notes that she had taken during the message to me.

Eventually Felicia talked me into going to that church on Wednesday nights. It was more of a Bible study. I was reluctantly open to the idea. I was introduced to more sound Bible teaching and had some things spoken to me, by the pastor, from a prophetic standpoint. This was a clue to me that the Lord was calling my name and saying, "It is time." I repented of my misdeeds and turned my life over to Christ. I did that in the privacy of my living room. I did not have a church service altar call moment. I had a Jesus moment! We joined the church and began attending regularly in 2009.

The only thing missing was my personal Bible study. I just did not believe I could read it for myself and understand it. But, I knew I had to try. I looked on my book shelf where I knew a few Bibles had been collecting dust. On the shelf I found a brand new Bible that was still in its initial box. The binder read: "Life Application Study Bible." I noticed that it was the New Living Translation (NLT) which was unfamiliar to me. I already knew about the common ones like the New International Version (NIV) and the various King James versions. I also recognized that the Bible had been a Christmas gift to me several years earlier from my Aunt Julia. Clearly I was not interested in the gift when I received it. It had been sitting on my book shelf, forgotten.

The great thing about a study Bible is that it provides commentary and easy cross referencing. This Bible also had a one year Bible reading plan in the back. (I still have not found a better reading plan for a beginner than this one). This plan did not have me read every page of the Bible in a year. But it did have me hit the highlights of the Bible, from Genesis to Revelation, in a year. The story of the Bible slows down wherever it has long passages about lineage, laws, and judgments. For a beginner, Bible reading can become very mechanical and boring when things are read that do not seem to relate to the overall storyline. Furthermore, the NLT was written in a way that I could understand what I was reading. In other words, it did not seem like I was reading a Shakespearean tale of some sort. I was reading the Bible passages, the commentaries, and the cross referencing points that went along with it and I was hooked! My life was changed and it has not been the same since I found that Bible on my shelf.

The Journey Ahead:

The best things in life have a process connected to them and fully understanding the things of God is no different. I am asking you to allow me to lead you on a journey. For those of you who do not know very much about God and the Bible, the things you will read will be easier for you to digest. However, considering the opposite extreme, religious people will have a hard time with some of the concepts and truths that will be discussed. That is because, usually, once one believes something is true, they rarely go back and revisit the issue in order to test their current notion to see if it still holds up. For those people, I ask that you make a decision to put a hold on your feelings of offense and judgment and wait the process out before you make a complete decision.

THE BIBLE

Everything that we know and believe about God the Creator and Jesus the Christ, and how someone should respond to facts or beliefs concerning them, are all based on ancient scriptures of God, otherwise referred to as the Bible. One must trust the historical reliability of the Bible, as well as believe in its divine inspiration to know or believe correctly about God and Jesus. Only then, can one believe the Bible contains God's words to human beings.

Is the Bible what it claims to be? Why are Christians so certain that the Bible contains no errors, while critics attack it by highlighting its inaccuracies, contradictions, and misconceptions? Is the Bible just one of many religious pieces of literature that one can read or, does it stand alone somehow?

Many people have and will continue to denounce the Bible which proves that faith in God as Creator, Jesus as the unique Son of the Creator, and all they have to say to the world is dependent on the reliability and inspiration of the Bible.

The Bible does not contain all wisdom and knowledge ever known or discovered. It does contain all the knowledge necessary to bring one to know God, please Him, and inherit the kingdom of God. So, if the Creator of the universe had something to tell you wouldn't you want to listen, consider, and act upon those words?

If anyone does not want to believe everything the Bible declares is true, then they have to discount its origins, authorship, and transferability. Doing so would prove to them flaws exist and those "flaws," call all of its words into question for them. If the Bible is questionable then God and His unique Son are questionable as well. Therefore, besides faith, the Bible is the most important factor in choosing to know and love God and His Son, or choosing the opposite which is to live apart from God, His presence, and His wisdom.

I do not want to take the easy way out here. Most in my position would decide to use scripture to prove that the Bible is reliable and divinely inspired. However, if the *accuracy* and *inerrancy* of the Bible is in question, then using the word of God as its own proof is a weak argument and testimony.

You may ask, "Is there any proof that the Bible is what Christians say it is?" There is an abundant amount of proof. There is way too much proof for me to even attempt to cover it all in this book, but I do want to cover the basics with you.

The Bible is on trial in this world. It has been accused of lies, half-truths, and errors. Are any of these claims true? Are there good reasons for anyone to discount these claims and not believe in the God of the Bible? Is the Bible full of facts or myths? What is the difference between the Bible and all other readings that various religions have to offer? There seems to be a hung jury concerning all of these things. So, what will you decide?

Translation:

The Bible is a collection of writings. It took more than 40 authors and over 1500 years to amass the amount of material found in the Bible. The scriptures were originally written in 3 different languages: Hebrew, Aramaic, and Greek. This must be remembered since the Bible we read has been translated into our native tongue.

These three original languages have caused translators problems. The Aramaic language has been dead for many centuries. That makes it hard to understand since no one uses it anymore. The brand of Hebrew used died about 300 B.C. There is Modern Hebrew used now but it is very different from the old one. The Greek used in the Bible might be better called "ancient Greek." There is Modern Greek used today, but the changes between the two make them very different. Also, in ancient Aramaic and Hebrew writings, there were no vowels, capitalization, spacing, paragraphs, or punctuation used in the manuscripts. This is another problem when it comes to translating the material to English.

What if this were done in our language? Consider this sentence: ONEDAYTHELORDWILLRETURNWITHPOWERANDGLORY. If you think that is bad, check this one out: NDYTHLRDWLLRTRNWTHPWRNDGLRY. That just looks like nonsense, right?

Now consider there are no more original writings of the scriptures, only handwritten copies. That means none of them are exactly the same. Minor errors committed by the copyists have passed into print. However, the similarities between copies written in different places, eras, or languages is remarkable. This is why different Bible translations have certain scriptures where the meaning is not agreed upon.

Furthermore, the Bible was not written like a school textbook or encyclopedia. These embody only one type of nonfiction. In contrast, the Bible was written in many literary styles which include poetry, biography, law, allegory, satire, and more. Depending on which style you are reading, the meaning of the text is affected. Therefore, translation and interpretation are closely related to each other. Both affect the other, so the Bible you choose is very important.

My advice to you is to pick one translation as your primary study. This will aide in memorization. But when it comes to scriptures that are hard to understand or need further insight, read different translations. This is very important! If five translations have a scripture basically saying the same thing, then you know you have the right interpretation. However, if those five do not agree with each other then you know the scripture was hard to translate or interpret. Reading five different translations may be good enough to enlighten your understanding but further study may be necessary by using a Bible commentary (a systematic set of explanations and interpretations of scripture) for that particular book. By the way, THERE IS NO REPLACEMENT FOR THE HOLY SPIRIT IN YOUR LIFE HELPING YOU DISCERN WHAT GOD IS TRYING TO SAY TO YOU THROUGH SCRIPTURE! Do not forget that.

You may hear people saying that only the King James Version (KJV) or the New International Version (NIV) is the only good Bible to use. Any comment like this regarding these two translations or any other translation is complete nonsense! You must be mindful of the translation you are using but pick one that is good for you.

There are basically three translations: literal, dynamic, and free. Literal translations try to stay as close to the original language as possible. The down side of that is the actual meaning from the author is lost to modern readers and can defeat the purpose.

Dynamic translations try to stay close to the original language as well but do not want the original meaning to be lost so they add words and idioms to make the wording closer to modern language without taking too many liberties.

Free translations are usually called paraphrases. They are more concerned with transferring the original idea as opposed to the literal wordings. Paraphrases are the exact opposite of literal versions. Paraphrases place a high regard to ideas while literal versions place a high regard to word for word translation regardless of the possibility of original ideas being lost. Paraphrases are easy to read and understand, maybe too easy. Literals can be hard to understand. More importantly, literals can be intimidating which can cause someone to not want to read the Bible at all.

Dynamics are the best of both worlds. They are easier to understand than the literals while trying to stay close to the original wording as possible. King James Version is probably the most rigid of all while the Message is probably the most free or loose of all.

What are my favorites? I will read anything, but I prefer New Revised Standard Version (NRSV) for my dynamic, New Living Translation (NLT) for my paraphrase, and the New King James Version (NKJV) for my literal. Choose wisely and pray for the Holy Spirit to give knowledge and understanding.

Interpretation:

Interpretation is about the way one comes to understand something. So how should we interpret what we read in the Bible? The historical context of what was going on within the storyline and the author is very important. Knowing if there was war or peace, famine or plenty, or any other thing with historical significance can aide in discovering the author's influence and purpose for writing the text. Understanding the cultural context is also vital.

The customs, habits, and traditions of the biblical writers definitely influenced them so texts should always be read with that in mind. Literary context is important too since the original writers did not separate the texts into chapters or verses. Therefore, every verse must be read in light of its context which consists, in the least the entire chapter, and at most the entire book.

Beware of any verse read or recited to you by itself. Always go and fact check the usage of the verse by reading it within the original context. Many doctrines have been falsely invented due to misused Bible verses which would have been better understood in light of the entire book!

The Bible often uses figurative speech. One must use careful study to discern when this is taking place. The problem is the reader cannot hear the tone the writer is using. This makes interpretation very difficult. Figures of speech (e.g., Isaiah 1:1-31) that are used include personifications (something non-human is given human qualities), similes or metaphors (comparisons), euphemisms (understatements), or hyperbole (exaggerations) [e.g., Luke 14:25-33]. These are easy to notice when listening to someone speak. However, without tone or facial expressions, the biblical text can be misinterpreted.

Next, we must discuss the use of parables and allegories. Parables are short fictional stories (e.g., Matthew 13:24-30). Jesus used parables often. It is important to know that parables are only meant to convey one main point and are not meant to be over analyzed. This can lead to false doctrines. Allegories are stories that have a figurative meaning (e.g., John 10:1-16). The Bible always gives proper analysis for the allegories. Refrain from adding a personal interpretation of an allegory that the Bible has already explained for you.

Genesis is a story that involves literal history and it is to be read plainly or from a historical perspective. However, Genesis should not be taken literally line-for-line. Genesis 2:7 speaks of God walking in the Garden. However, we know that God the Creator is Spirit and does not have a body or legs to "walk" on (John 4:24). So God's walking in the Garden with man, does not mean that He had literal legs, but that He and man communed with each other on a daily basis. How literal and figurative should we take Genesis? That's a subject for another day. Just use God's gift of discernment to help you along the way (1 Corinthians 2:10-16). Also, Genesis is not written from a scientific point of view. It uses prescientific language. Science does not discount Genesis any more than Genesis discounts science.

The main idea is that God the Creator is the ultimate cause of all things during creation. The creation account is to give us the true beginning of all things so that we can properly discern the information that science offers. For example, if two people receive directions that read, "Go 2 blocks north, then turn left for one mile." the assumption is that both people are starting from the same place. But if one of the people started 7 blocks south of the other, then they would end up in a completely different place. Their final destination would be the wrong location even though they followed the directions correctly.

The beginning of creation is from God the Creator. Any other beginning hypothesis will lead you to misinterpret the facts of science and lead you in the wrong direction. Furthermore, Genesis, as with other sections of the Old Testament, is not written in chronological order. This is another characteristic of ancient writing style. For instance, in Genesis chapter 1 God creates man, yet seems to do it again in chapter 2. The truth is that the same event is discussed in chapters 1 and 2 except from different perspectives.

The book of Revelation may be seen similarly. Revelation deals with a definite reality, whether in the past or future, even if the book cannot be taken literally.

Poetry is throughout the Old Testament. The book of Psalms is the most popular. Proverbs, Job, Song of Solomon (Song of Songs in some versions), Ecclesiastes, and others have poetry as a major or minor part of their narratives as well. It is best to read these parts of the Bible with a poetic mindset much like you did when you attended grade school.

Poetry is different than other narratives and needs to be read with a more imaginative and open minded thought process. Otherwise, you can misinterpret the text and be led astray. Raw human emotions like mourning, celebration, fear, and thanksgiving are expressed. This shouldn't be ignored while interpreting the texts. One must note that Hebrew poetry and Western poetry are not written the same way. Biblical poetry will not read like a nursery rhyme. Choose a Bible that writes poetry in stanza form, that way you will know when to put your "poetry hat" on.

The wisdom books include Job, Proverbs, and Ecclesiastes. Song of Solomon (Song of Songs), and Psalms have parts that could be considered wisdom narrative as well. One major mistake is to take in these scriptures in small doses rather than the whole context before forming an interpretation. Remember, the overall message is most important. Maybe the book of Proverbs can be taken in small doses, sense it is written in short, catchy, easy to remember lines, but beware! This book is meant to convey the basic wisdom of life. Therefore, it is not a legal guarantee from God but a guideline for good behavior.

Some verses reflect ancient culture and need to be interpreted for our day and time properly. Proverbs uses figurative language designed to be memorable and practical, not necessarily technically or theologically precise.

The verses should be weighed with other scriptures in the Bible before an interpretation is formed. The other wisdom books are written differently than Proverbs. The most important thing is to read the books in their full context and weigh them with other historical and theological parts of scripture.

Transferability:

The scriptures were written on perishable materials during ancient times such as papyrus, parchment, and vellum. That means the writings had to be copied over and over again until the invention of the printing press. These were not written in book form like we can see today. These writings were on scrolls that could be rolled up. However, the writing materials that I have mentioned were very rare, so the context of these writings had to be taught, learned, and passed on by word of mouth. Considering this, most would assume the original writings would change over time due to this primary mode of transfer. However, in this culture the Rabbis were known for memorizing the entire Old Testament and doing so accurately.

I know that sounds unbelievable but people of oral cultures have memories that are more reliable than most of ours. They did not have cell phones with google, copy machines, or desktop computers. Sophisticated memorization strategies were used to exercise their capacity to remember things. When these teachers would cite the scriptures from memory, if any part seemed to be wrong, inaccurate, or mistaken, the people would immediately call them on it. Memorization, back then, meant as long as the main essence of the story stayed the same, the rest could be paraphrased.

Every story had fixed points that wouldn't change. This explains why the Gospels (Matthew, Mark, Luke, John) tell the same story but are quite different in many ways. But remember, these stories came from eyewitness accounts. If they would have been the same verbatim then that would have brought their validity into question since no two people remember facts in the same way.

Reliability:

Is the Bible reliable? This question can be better stated by asking, "Is the Bible historically reliable," because that is what we are really asking here. If the Bible is bona fide history, then the claims it makes about God's Story should be reliable too. All historical documents are tested by a certain criteria to determine their historical reliability. The Bible should be tested by the exact same methods of criticism.

We have already covered what some call the "biographical test," which is how the text is transmitted over time. Next one should examine the internal and external evidence.

First of all, the Bible should be given the benefit of the doubt when one considers the longevity of these ancient manuscripts and how people have trusted them over a vast amount of time. The bottom line is, of all the so called "problems" of scripture that the Bible has been accused of, almost all of it has been explained in a satisfactory manner using the scripture itself or archaeological discoveries. Regarding archaeological findings, no discovery has ever dis-proven a biblical reference.

The New Testament was written on the basis of eyewitness accounts. Even in today's time, eyewitness account can be used in a court of law. For instance, if 5000 people saw a man commit a crime, physical evidence would not be necessary for the man to be found guilty. The same weight should be given to the biblical eyewitness account. And, by the way, there were many non-Christian historians during the first century who all corroborate the New Testament biblical account. Maybe the most well-known was a Pharisee and Jewish historian named Josephus. He verifies what the eyewitnesses were claiming even though he did not buy their story since he was a Jew.

Josephus and other historians confirm Jesus as a historical figure. Therefore, one's choice regarding Jesus should be about whether or not He is the Son of God, and not if He was a real person who claimed to be, and who many thought was the Son of God. Jesus is not like Santa Claus whose story originates with a real life person, a monk named St. Nicholas, who became the subject and central figure for many legends. The four Gospels are the primary sources for the life of Christ but the non-Christian's sources do confirm that Jesus was a wise and good man from Nazareth who was crucified. His disciples fully believed that He was raised from the dead. What many of the awesome feats the non-believers witnessed Jesus perform and called "sorcery," Christians called them "miracles." His disciples increased exponentially after His death. These facts can be confirmed outside of the biblical record.

The discrepancies in the Bible may seem to be real or true but are not necessarily so. There are many ways to deal with these issues. First, we should deal with difficult passages in the light of clear ones and within their full context. Next, general statements do not guarantee overarching promises from God. Finally, later revelation trumps previous revelation. There are more devices to use but these form a good starting point.

Inspiration:

The Bible contains writings from original manuscripts which were inspired by God. After considering all the facts, one must make a decision on whether or not they believe this statement. This is when faith becomes necessary.

The Bible claims God's inspiration for itself. So far I have not used scripture as factual evidence. This was to avoid something called circular reasoning. In other words, some would frown upon the Word of God, the Bible, being its own evidence for Godly inspiration. But why? Is self-authentication worthy evidence to prove the reliability of a statement or set of statements from the quoted author? We actually use this type of argument all the time! When we say, "I think...,"or "I believe...," we are making a statement that no one can prove beyond a shadow of a doubt. We all take turns "self-proofing" our statements to each other.

If you tell me that the L.A. Lakers are a good basketball team but I tell you, "I don't think that is true," then you have to honor my statement just as much as I must honor yours. When the subject matter seems to be subjective in its nature who can be right?

This is why it is typically easy to stump a Christian who is trying to tell someone about Jesus Christ by simply saying, "I don't believe in that," or "I think the Bible is full of mythology." These remarks are hard to overcome. The assumption is that the person's statements are fully reasonable, responsible, and fully reliable therefore, must be taken into evidence. But this simply is not true!

If mankind is fully reliable then our testimonies could be used exclusively in a court of law and exclude all other testimonies on the matter. Our testimonies or statements do not stand by themselves because we are sinful beings and by nature are not reliable or trustworthy.

Jesus agreed that self-authentication is unreliable when He said in John 5:31-32, "If I were to testify on my own behalf, my testimony would not be valid. But someone else is also testifying about me, and I assure you that everything he says about me is true." That "someone else" that Jesus speaks of is His Father, God the Creator. Since God created the universe and everything in it, don't we have to believe what He says?

If we cannot believe the Creator, then no other statement by anyone can be taken as truth. If that is the case that means there is no such thing as truth. And if that is the case YOU, nor I, should say another word about anything because we are all false witnesses!

One day Jesus made a claim about Himself when He professed to be "the light of the world," (John 8:12). Some religious people immediately refuted His statement by insisting that such a testimony is not valid (John 8:13). However, we know that Jesus is God (John 1:1-5) and Jesus appropriately declared in John 8:14, "These claims are valid even though I make them about myself. For I know where I came from and where I am going, but you don't know this about me."

The Bible claims to be God's words to mankind in 2 Timothy 3:16, "All Scripture is inspired by God and is useful to teach us what is true and to make us realize what is wrong in our lives. It corrects us when we are wrong and teaches us to do what is right." A psalmist agrees when he says, "And the words of the Lord are flawless, like silver purified in a crucible, like gold refined seven times." (Psalm 12:6; NIV). Therefore, since Jesus' claims about Himself are a worthy testimony, then the Bible's claims about itself, God's word, must be seen as an authoritative and final testimony for all to consider.

Inerrancy and Infallibility:

This brings me to my main and most important point of all. But first let me say that God the Creator is perfect. It should not be hard to consider the maker of the entire universe as perfect, right? If God the Father existed before anything else, then everything made must be compared to the One who was always around. This is how we discover our sin in comparison to God. If there is such a thing as perfection, then the One who has made all things must be how one would measure perfection. In other words, we only know our failures by comparing ourselves to others or by standards created by others.

If God existed before anyone else, then there would be no one available for comparison. A flaw or imperfection cannot exist where there is no better measure to judge by. So if God is perfect then so are His words! That being said, I want to introduce two terms: inerrancy and infallibility.

Christians often describe the Bible using these two words. To say the Word of God is inerrant is to say that it is without error. To say the Word of God is infallible is to say that it is impossible for it to have any error. The Bible contains the Word of God. Now just to be clear, inerrancy and infallibility does not mean everything in the Bible is true since men have lied therein, including Satan. But the records of such events are accurate. Inerrancy and infallibility does not mean contradiction does not seem to be in the text however, this can be resolved. Inerrancy and infallibility does not mean the copies of the Bible or manuscripts are without error.

Remember the original copies, which are without error, are lost just like every other original ancient writing in history. However, the text has been amazingly preserved through copies and word of mouth. Lastly, inerrancy and infallibility does not mean the many writers of the scriptures were perfect people without error. In fact, they were sinful people. But the words they wrote in scripture were divinely inspired by God and are without error. This is because the Holy Spirit worked in them and did not allow errors to creep into their writings.

The writers used their own mind which was formed through personal experience, culture, style, and other factors, but the Holy Spirit made sure they accurately recorded everything God wanted them to say in spite of their personalities. Indeed, the inerrancy of Scripture involves the harmony of God and man. Since the writers spoke and wrote God's Word (Deuteronomy 18:18 and Jeremiah 1:9), then their writings are inerrant and infallible as the author.

The Bible is the inerrant and infallible Word from God to mankind. This is important to know and believe because if the Word of God is flawed in anyway then everything it says and claims are in question and therefore, it's author, the Creator and Christ are in question too. If we cannot believe everything the Bible says, we cannot believe everything that God says, which means He is not flawless. This is not true! Belief in the inerrancy and infallibility of the Bible gives us confidence in the truth of the gospel no matter what is happening in our world, environment, or lives.

The Bible gives us confidence that Christ is who He says He is, no matter what the world has to say about Him. It gives us confidence that supports science and not the other way around. When the world claims Darwinism and such, then we know they are false! It gives us confidence that God's inerrant and infallible Word can still be preached today in spite of our opinions and misconceptions because we have it in black and white. We can also know if any preaching is flawed by comparison to the Scriptures. We have confidence that the same God who revealed Himself to the first humans on earth has revealed Himself to us as well!

Without the supreme authority of Scripture, the gospel is like a domestic cat without his claws. If you have ever been around a declawed cat before then you know just how weak they are. Their claws are the only source of power they have. When the cat pounces on you, its paws feel like pillows. Useless! The Bible would be the same way if not for the fact that its words have been inspired by God, which makes it without and incapable of error. Thank God for His words to us! He has given us specific instructions for our lives. The Creator of the universe has spoken!

The Cannon:

As a collection of writings or books, the Bible does not contain every Christian book ever written in antiquity. Instead a select group of books were chosen. Many refer to these chosen books as the "Canon" which means, "an officially accepted list of books." The books that were chosen to be in the Bible were considered to be inspired by God, the others were not.

Some of the books came close to being chosen but they did not fit the established criteria. The guidelines for being accepted included but were not limited to: it was written by a prophet, performed miracles confirm the writer, the power of God was perceived in the writings, it was acceptable by the people of God, or the writing did not contain known falsehoods.

The most popular of the writings not chosen to be included in the Canon are known as "The Apocrypha." These books were added to the Old Testament by the Roman Catholic Church. Inaccuracies, false doctrines, and prophetic power are just some of the reasons these books were not chosen to be in the Bible. The characteristics of the Bible are multi-faceted. Considering this Hebrews 4:12 is a great place to see these characteristics condensed into an easily digestible format. Read this chapter in its full context before concentrating on verse 12. We can see one main attribute here. Let's break it down.

First, the Word of God is living. 1 Peter 1:23 confirms this as true. Furthermore, many times the Bible describes God the

Creator as a living God. Hebrews 3:12, 9:14, 10:31, and 12:22 are just a few places in the New Testament that speak to this fact. The Author of the Bible is living and so are His words. The ink on the page is just material. But when those words are read or spoken, they take on a life of their own, literally! We also know from the creation story in Genesis that life begets life. The Word of God brings life to the hearer. Secondly, the Word of God is powerful. It is so powerful that a person's heart can be changed as if it were once made of stone, but then was miraculously made pliable (Ezekiel 36:26). Read the imagery in Jeremiah 23:29 that illustrates God's power through His Word. I cannot list all that its power can perform. Ultimately, God's Word will negotiate the fall of Satan's kingdom and set up the kingdom of Christ here on earth, a feat which has already begun invisibly in the spirit realm.

Third, the Word of God is sharp. The scripture wants you to picture a sword here so that you might understand its ability to divide things. Just like a sword can divide the body, joint and marrow, the Bible can divide soul and spirit. Your soul is basically how you think and feel here on earth. Your spirit, upon salvation, is one with Christ (2 Corinthians 5:8). The Word of God can fully distinguish between your soul, who you are apart from Christ, and your spirit, that which has been taken over by the Holy Spirit Himself.

We are to become more and more like Christ every day (Romans 8:29) and the Bible helps us do that. It exposes our deepest thoughts and desires. The Word of God shows us who God is. Only then can we see who we are apart from God. By His power, we can change and move closer to being like God intended us to be.

The Bible gives us discernment. When we learn to critique ourselves by the scriptures and help from the Holy Spirit, we can begin to shift that discernment other places like people, false doctrine, and circumstances. Christ is the mediator between God the Creator and man. Without Christ here in the flesh, it can be hard to discern what the Holy Spirit is saying to us, so we use the Word of God, the Bible.

Why read the Bible? Without faith, it is impossible to please God (Hebrews 11:6)! There is a clear way that we can receive faith in which to please God. Faith comes by reading or hearing the Word of God (Romans 10:17). Reading the Bible is absolutely essential and necessary for one's walk with Christ. Reading the Bible to receive faith is a general reason for personal study in God's Word. Now let's discuss some specific reasons for doing so.

The Bible reveals God's will for our lives. When we pray, we should talk about God's will for our lives. The Bible is how one can discover what that is. It cannot tell you who to marry, what occupation to seek, or anything specific like that. Those questions are for the Holy Spirit to answer for you. However, the Holy Spirit can use the Bible to divide soul and spirit, what we want from what God wants, which can heighten our abilities of discernment so we can discover God's heart regarding a certain situation or our direction.

Reading the Bible will nourish you. Just like you need food to live, upon salvation, you need spiritual food to live. That is the Word of God. The spirit gives life and God's Word is spirit (John 6:63). Furthermore, Jesus cited an Old Testament scripture when He said, "People do not live by bread alone, but by every word that comes from the mouth of God." Therefore, people need food to eat, both physical and spiritual. Your body needs food. Your spirit needs the Word of God. I know I have stated this several times now but it bears repeating. Reading the Bible gives us discernment.

We have already studied Hebrews 4:12, now let's read Isaiah 55:8: "My thoughts are nothing like your thoughts… And my ways are far beyond anything you could imagine." In order to take on the mind of Christ (1 Corinthians 2:16), we have to know what He is thinking. The Word of God reveals that to us. With this information, we can use discernment in our everyday lives. Discernment is the ability to judge well. We should not judge people with condemnation (Matthew 7:1) but we can judge actions, relationships, intentions, environments, circumstances, and other stuff by using discernment. The Word of God, along with the Holy Spirit, will develop this skill in you.

The Bible teaches us how to be righteous (2 Timothy 3:16-17). Many people see the word "righteousness" as a religious term. But it is a legal term. To be righteous simply means to be rightly aligned or in good standing with God.

How do we become righteous? Our eternal righteousness comes from Christ (Romans 3:22). He takes His own perfection, or righteousness, and bestows it upon all who believe in spite of their sins. When God the Creator sees a man/woman in Christ, He does not see their imperfections, only Christ's perfections upon them. We are called to live out a righteous or moral life in which we seek to obey God's laws and ways for us. The way we learn how to live a life that pleases God is by reading His Word for us.

Furthermore, we have to have faith to please God (Hebrews 11:6; Romans 10:17) and we have to know God to please Him (2 Peter 1:3). We can accomplish both by reading the Bible.

God's Word has POWER, another previously mentioned characteristic, for the believer to use to overcome many different issues of life, including temptation. It takes God's power in your life to overcome temptation.

Jesus used the Word of God as a weapon while He was tempted in the wilderness (Matthew 4:1-11). This is must read material! Ephesians 6:17 confirms how God's Word can be used to defeat the enemy who tempts us. The passage uses the same imagery we read in Hebrews 4:12. A sword was a normal weapon used in ancient times. Jesus fought with this weapon

44

while alone, weak, and hungry in the desert. It caused Satan himself to flee.

We are all tempted in many ways to go against the ways of God. God will show you a way out of temptation (1 Corinthians 10:13) and one way He does that is with His Word. All of these things involve God's power. The Bible will help you harness it for yourself.

I cannot list here all that the Bible is useful for. I have given you some general categories and subcategories that further, and more specifically, list reasons to read the Bible. The Bible contains all of God's promises to man which, if one knows what they are, can be leaned on during times of hardship and trial. The Bible answers many of the tough questions of life that are so hard to figure out like, "What is the meaning of life?", "How did life begin?", "Why does a loving God allow evil in the world?", "Why is it hard to be a good person?", and "Who is God?" Read the Bible for yourself and reap the rewards therein!

THE GOSPEL: THE KINGDOM OF GOD

You have probably heard about the gospel. To many people, the gospel just refers to subject matter that is discussed in church or in the Bible. Basically, many people think the word "gospel" is just another religious word. In fact "gospel," does not refer to religion at all. So what does this word actually mean? Gospel very simply means "good news." That's it. The question that needs to be asked is "What is the good news?" In Matthew 4:23 (among other verses) we see the answer: "Jesus traveled throughout the region of Galilee, teaching in the synagogues and announcing the Good News about the Kingdom. And he healed every kind of disease and illness."

Some translations use the word gospel instead of good news, but one can see the phrase refers to a kingdom. What kingdom is this passage referring to exactly? Verse 14 says "From then on Jesus began to preach, 'Repent of your sins and turn to God, for the Kingdom of Heaven is near."' In comparison Jesus said in Mark 1:15 "The Kingdom of God is near! Repent of your sins and believe the Good News!" Therefore, the "kingdom of God," and the "kingdom of heaven," refer to the same thing, which is the good news.

Jesus was not the only one in the Bible to speak of this good news. But what is the kingdom of God (heaven), and what is so good about it? I have no idea where you are in your walk with Christ today, whether you are a new person in Christ or have been for years, but get ready to open up your mind and heart. This may be the first time you have ever heard about the true gospel mentioned in the Bible. As the Lord reveals to you this "mystery," all things of God will open up to you.

The gospel that Jesus, John the Baptist, and the other apostles refer to in the Bible is not about the cross that Jesus died on. We love to talk about the cross and wear it as pendants on our bodies, but it does not refer to the gospel. The gospel is not about the blood of Jesus. Christians have spoken and rejoiced about the blood spilled from the body of Jesus for the remission of sins for thousands of years. There is power in the blood of Jesus, but that is not the gospel. The gospel is not about going to heaven. If one repents and believes in Jesus, then when they die, heaven will be their destination, but that is not the gospel. The gospel is not about going to church and being a good person. The Bible talks about the people of God communing together and growing to be more and more like

Christ, but that is not the gospel. The gospel is not about love. God loves us so much that we cannot measure it. We are to love God above all else. We are commanded to love our neighbor as He loved us. But that is not the gospel. What is the gospel? The arrival of the kingdom of God is the good news!

Jesus did not come to the earth to start a religion. Religion is what one does to try and get close to God or win His approval. Religion is how one tries to get God to like them or perform for them. Religion is hard work. The word religion means bondage. Jesus came to "set the captives free" (Luke 4:18), "and who the Son sets free is absolutely free" (John 8:36).

The next thing that I am going to say may sound very radical to you but...here it goes. CHRISTIANITY IS A RELIGION! There...I said it. Yes, I use the word "Christian" to describe myself and my beliefs because it is a word that everyone understands. Similarly, I use the word "church" to describe the place I attend on Sundays to worship with the people of God and hear His word, even though I know the place I attend is not church at all. A church is not a building (I'll discuss this more later). Yet I still use the word because people are used to it and can understand where I am going. So, why do I say that Christianity is a religion? It's supposed to be taught and directed by using one book, the Bible, so why are there so many denominations, factions, and subsidiaries of what we call Christianity? How is one book so divisive among the people who claim to be brothers and sisters who follow and hear from the same Lord? I think it's because people like to figure out their own way into God's graces even though we are all supposed to believe in only ONE WAY!

Take a step back and look at Christianity. There seems to be many different ways. That's religion. In some ways Christianity looks like any other religion on the planet in that they are all trying to get to God. The Christians, Jews, and Muslims, to name a few, can't even agree on who Jesus is or is not! So, when a Christian tries to tell someone that the only way is Jesus, it sounds foolish. Who is Jesus anyway? Do most people even know? Meanwhile, all religions want the same thing...to live forever and have significance in the universe, and with so many religious options, how can anyone choose?

When somebody is introduced to Christianity they see it as just one option on a buffet line. How does one pick a T-bone steak over a Prime Rib? Imagine standing at the taco bar, all American bar, salad bar, or dessert bar and thinking "It all looks so good! There is only so much room on my plate! How do I decide? And what about the drinks? Let's see...there is soda, tea, coffee, milk, juice, and several versions of each." In this scenario most would agree that all of the choices available have their pros and cons, but people are told to do whatever feels good to them so what difference does it make, right? But of course, there are those people who, due to the mass amount of choice, decide to pick nothing at all. They feel like they have been set free by not making a decision, and therefore, are not bound to the consequence of making the wrong choice. These people just go hungry and end up feeding on any trash they can find, or that is presented to them.

Let's look at it another way. Imagine you are sitting at a table with friends and family and enjoying a meal together. The subject of religion comes up and everyone starts discussing their belief systems. The first person at the table speaks first and says "I believe that Muhammad brought God's final revelation to man. God is unknowable. He doesn't want a relationship with us but He does want us to know His will. I work very hard to be a good person and please God so I can make it to heaven." The second person speaks up and says "I believe the sacred scriptures of the Vedas which says that truth is eternal and the very essence of the universe. Brahman is the all-powerful and true God. I want to be a good person so I can achieve dharma. A person's soul never dies. It just goes to another body. Maybe one day I can achieve moksha and live with Brahman forever!" Imagine that you are still sitting at the table silently listening while you eat.

The third person speaks up and says "Buddha teaches that there is no supreme God. I just want to achieve enlightenment by being a good person. That way I will not find bad karma. Through reincarnation, I'll never die. Who knows where I'll be in the next life." Then a fourth one begins to speak and says "I believe in the teachings of Confucius. I don't believe in gods but I do walk in the path of righteousness. All people are good and then learn to do bad things later on. I believe in mercy and goodwill for all mankind." And still a fifth person says "I believe in the one true God of Israel. The ancient writings of the Torah are my main source of information. God is loving, kind, and faithful. Christians try to throw Jesus into the picture. He was just a good teacher, maybe a prophet at best. The true Messiah will come one day and liberate Israel." The sixth person says "I don't believe in any of that stuff! I just live my life and do what I want to do. I am the judge of what is good or bad. If it doesn't hurt anybody then how bad can it be? If there is a god, I don't know him. But I know you guys!"

Finally it is your turn to speak. You finish your last swallow of food and say, "I am a Christian. I believe in Jesus as Lord and Savior of the world. Whoever believes in Him will live forever. I try to be a good person but never get it completely right. However, Jesus is my righteousness and pathway to God. The Bible tells me I can talk to God as one would to a friend."

The table is full of different beliefs. From the outside looking in, what is the difference? Let's continue to pretend that the statement about your beliefs, which is about being a Christian, is all that you said. You just stated your beliefs along with all the others and left it at that. Well, why say any more than that? They stated their beliefs and you stated your beliefs. You don't have to believe what they believe and they don't have to believe what you believe, right? No wonder Christianity can seem like just any other religion or just another pot in the cabinet. But let's consider this. What if, out of all the belief systems at the table, only one was actually true? If this was the case, then that fact would downgrade all the other beliefs into being no more significant than the lies that many of us believed at some point or another about Santa Claus, the Easter Bunny, Tooth Fairy, leprechaun, Boogie Man, or Cupid. Most would have died in defense of the belief only to discover that it was not true. What am I saying? Just because you believe in something does not make it true! Let that soak in for a second.

Let's get back to our scenario for a minute. As we know it, Christianity can seem just like any other religion and in many ways it is, but Jesus did not come to start a religion. He came to make an announcement and then fulfill that announcement by who He was and what He did on the planet. Now, should the Christian at the table reveal to their friends and family that their beliefs don't matter because they are not true? If not, they might as well rekindle their belief system in Santa Claus or the Tooth Fairy because all of those lies get you the same thing… nothing! Or, at least they won't get you the ability to live forever or be of any significance in the universe. If that is the case then why believe in it? Well, because they think, or believe their belief is true. But it's not.

So what is the gospel message? It is very simple to understand. You do not need to go to seminary to understand it nor be a pastor. Everyone has the ability to understand it. In fact, Jesus makes this point very clear when He said in Mark 4:11

"You are permitted to understand the secret of the Kingdom of God." The secret can be revealed to anyone by God Himself if they repent of their ways, believe in the Son, and ask for wisdom. Generally, people who are not religious will take to the gospel that Jesus preached a lot easier than religious people because a religious person must unlearn everything they were taught before the gospel message can be digested properly. This can be an overwhelming undertaking but anything is possible with God!

The Gospel is like a pizza:

Now...am I saying that the religious Christian message is all lies? No, of course not! Let me tell you like this. The Kingdom of God is like a pizza. What is a pizza? What is it made out of? A pizza consists of cheese, bread, sauce, numerous topping options, and spices. The bread represents Jesus, the bread of life, as the foundation of the pizza. Everything depends on it to be in the right place. The sauce represents His blood which came from His body and was poured out for the remission of sin. The cheese is the word of God. Its only job is to reveal what lies underneath, the mystery of Jesus Christ. The cheese holds up the toppings. The toppings are the many pieces of information or teachings about the kingdom of God that we need to know and learn so we can have full understanding at our disposal. Unfortunately, many people prefer certain toppings over others which dilute the intended wholesomeness of the pizza.

Indeed, all of the toppings serve their purpose and are equally important. The spices are the people of God. The spices provide the flavor to the pizza, like salt on a potato chip. Without the spices, the pizza grows bland and has no power or flavor in it. The pizza exists without the spices. However, the spices have the job of unlocking the flavor or the power of the kingdom of God on the earth. What is next? The oven of course. Nobody wants to eat a raw pizza. The baking is important because it blends everything together. The baking represents our trials and tribulation on the planet earth. Heat or fire can kill but God uses it for His glory. Each ingredient is able to become what it was truly destined to be. When the bread raises up after the sauce and heat are put all over it, it then raises up everything else with it. Indeed, the ingredients glorify the bread. Yet, all together they make up the kingdom of God on the planet earth. After baking, the pizza seems irresistible to the senses. Now, who's hungry?!

The kingdom of God is like a pizza. But some people do not like to take it in all at once. So they pull off the sausage and eat it. Then they pull off the pepperoni and eat it. Then they pull off the cheese and eat it. And finally the bread and sauce is consumed, if they are not full already. I have seen many children eat pizza this way but they rarely make it to the bread and sauce before they are disinterested and move on to something else. That way of consuming the pizza represents religion. Religion takes the cheese and tries to sell it to you as the pizza or it takes the pepperoni and tries to do the same. Religion can even take the bread and sell it as the pizza.

If I invite someone over to my house to eat pizza, but I tell them we're having sausage, would they be confused when they arrive and see a pizza with sausage on it sitting on the table? They would probably wonder out loud "I thought we were eating sausage." My reply might be "We are eating sausage." Their comment would undoubtedly be "No we're not. We are going to eat a pizza that has sausage on it! They are not the same thing." In this instance, religion over emphasized the sausage and set it apart, even though God wants the whole pizza to be presented and delivered. The gospel or good news, is about the fullness of the pizza. It is not about any of the ingredients placed by themselves or over emphasized. This is very important. God wants you to know about and eat the entire pizza. Bon appetit!

The Kingdom of God:

In the first book of the Bible, Genesis, we can read about how God created the heavens and the earth. In other words, God created everything you can see and everything you can't see. Notice that God created more than just one heaven. The Bible speaks of three separate heavens. In Genesis 6:7 God is referring to the birds of heaven. Some Bible translations have decided not to use the word "heaven" and instead use the word "sky". That way the reader can better understand what the passage is talking about. The original Hebrew word used here is "shamayim," which is the same original word for "heaven" we read in the first verse recorded in the Bible which referred to more than one heaven. Genesis 6:7, therefore, refers to the first heaven which we call the sky.

The second heaven is actually outer space. We can read in Matthew 24:29 when Jesus talked about stars falling from the sky. Again, some translations use "sky" while older ones use "heaven". This does not speak of the heaven that birds fly in. This heaven holds the planets and stars in space. The third heaven is often referred to as the highest heaven. This is where God resides. God cannot be contained in one place yet the Bible does refer to Him and His dwelling place. Hebrews 8:1 speaks of the High Priest (Jesus) sitting down on the throne next to God in heaven. This heaven is above the sky and outer space. It is the highest heaven. Notice there are thrones up there. Who sit on thrones? Kings do, of course. Therefore, in heaven, God is the King. Many scriptures refer to God as King. All kings have a domain that they rule over. A government is made out of a king's rulership over his domain.

It is important to know that a kingdom is not like a democracy. A democracy is for the people and by the people. But a kingdom is for the king and by the king. So democracy and any kingdom (including God's) are polar opposites of each other. Therefore, a king owns everything held within his domain. This includes the land, everything that sits on the land, and even the people. I want to stress that the kingdom of God is a government. Its headquarters are in the highest heaven. There are no other earthly governments that compare to it. Even the earthly kingdoms of the past cannot compare to it since their kings were not righteous, wise, benevolent, powerful, wealthy, sincere, or loving enough to contend with the rulership of God and His kingdom. God's army is even stronger than any earthly army which means He can conquer any nation whenever He sets His mind to do it! Are you with me so far? Let's continue.

If you are unfamiliar, you may want to take a minute and read the first three chapters of Genesis. This will aid your understanding as I continue to explain the kingdom of God. Don't worry. It is real easy reading. Not long at all. Many mysteries are held within those first three chapters. Anyway, what are you doing? Go ahead and read. I will wait.

Kingdom Expansion:

God had one thing in mind when He created the earth. That was to extend His kingdom, which is in heaven, down to earth. God's idea was to literally have heaven on earth. Why did God create human beings? Well it was not because He was lonely or needed people to love. God does not need anything but Himself. He made humans for the purpose of ruling His kingdom on earth. God made humans in His image to be like Him (Gen. 1:26). God is a Ruler. Therefore, so is man. Man is supposed to be royalty (1 Peter 2:9). Only those who are in the same bloodline as a king can be considered royalty. Psalms 82:6 says "You are gods; you are children of the Most High". Jesus even quoted this scripture in John 10:34 and said the scriptures cannot be altered. Notice that a lowercase "g" is used here. The scripture does not mean that we are equivalent to God. But we are similar to Him in certain ways. Back to Genesis 1:26…"they will reign…" Other translations use different words instead of "reign" like rule, dominion, power, or master. In verse 27 we were made in God's image. This does not mean we look like Him. God, the Father, does not have a body like Jesus or we do. The word "image" here refers to a resemblance to something, a shadow of something, or a representative figure for something. In verse 28 we can see the same word used in verse 26. But another word is introduced when the Lord tells us to govern (subdue, control, master) the earth. I like the NLT translation of "govern" sense it makes it plain that a government is involved.

Let's go back to verse 26. "They will reign", "They may…", or "Let them…" denotes an established contract between God and man. To help in our understanding let's consider the first century Roman government. They stayed clear of the title "king". Instead they had emperors. Their entire empire was made up of many different areas. So whoever the emperor was would establish a governor to rule the land on behalf of the emperor (since the emperor cannot be everywhere while ruling such a large empire). The governor has authority given to him by the emperor. A governor is placed in an area to facilitate the extension of the empire in a given land. That is exactly what happened in the account we read in Genesis. God wanted to extend His government to earth. He placed mankind there to rule it on His behalf. This means that man was not supposed to rule the earth in just anyway but man was to rule the earth however God wanted him to. Man did not establish the kingdom but God did. It was God's kingdom and man was given the authority to rule over it on God's behalf. Man's job was to work or serve the land by watching over, guarding, protecting, and subduing it so that the land may remain conformed to the precepts of the kingdom of God (Genesis 2:15). This meant tending to the animals which included naming them. But Adam's main job was to protect the area from any thought process that would seek to come against God's established way of life on earth. Adam and Eve never had children in the Garden of Eden. However, they would have taught the children to work in the same way.

God's creation was perfect before Adam and Eve sinned. That event is referred to as the "Fall of Man". Man was given a fierce warning (Gen. 2:16-17). Every tree in the garden was acceptable to eat from except the tree of the knowledge of good and evil. The consequence of ignoring this warning would be death! It is important to note that mankind was never originally designed to die (a commonality they would hold with their Creator).

Then the serpent, better known as the devil, shows up. Why did God allow him into the garden? So man would have a choice. God does not want mankind to be like robots who can only do what they are programmed to do. We have been given the freedom to choose against God. This is because God wants us to have true rulership. God wants us to be able to do whatever we want. However, His plan was that we would only want what He wants. So there is a tough quandary here. We were designed to rule the earth with our will. But our will was supposed to mirror or reflect God's will.

Here is another way of explaining this dynamic. If God is the sun then mankind is the moon. The moon's light comes from the sun which reflects off the moon. The awesome thing is that the moon appears to our eyes like it is producing light. It might as well be because that is what it looks like. But it's not. It just looks like it does. The light that it appears to have is not its own light. The light did not originate with the moon. It comes from the sun. It's the sun's light. It's almost like the moon uses the light to glorify the sun in a dark place. Likewise, mankind is to glorify the Creator as His will shines on us and we execute it on earth. Part of the execution will depend on the person since we are all made differently by God (on purpose). It is funny how there seems to be many moons. There are eight different ways that the moon reflects the sun's light. The sun never changes but how the moon reflects it does. The moon looks so different for every changing reflection that each one has a name from the crescent moon all the way to the half-moon. Therefore, God's character stays the same but people are different. Each person who accepts the will of God will reflect it differently. One way is not better than the other as long as God's will is reflected.

Intruder Alert:

The serpent enters into the garden in Genesis chapter three. He questioned Eve about what God said concerning the forbidden tree. After Eve tells of the death sentence upon eating from it, the serpent lies to her and claims "You won't die!" (Verse 4). Then the serpent twisted the truth. "God knows that your eyes will be opened as soon as you eat it, and you will be like God, knowing both good and evil." (Verse 5). Technically he was right but did not tell Eve that mankind was NEVER designed to understand evil. Man was only supposed to know what God wanted them to know. So Adam and Eve ate because the tree and its fruit looked good. Plus they wanted the extra knowledge due to the planted idea that they were missing out on something. Remember that Adam's job was to protect the garden from foreign ideas. He failed at this task.

Next the Bible says that their eyes were opened. That means Adam and Eve now understood things that they were never supposed to understand like shame and nakedness. These feelings were due to the fact that they were now thinking and acting contrary to God's will. So mankind was no longer

THE GOSPEL: THE KINGDOM OF GOD

perfect. Furthermore, God promised them they would die if they ate from the forbidden tree. It is important to note that whatever God promises He must perform. God will not go against His own words. Therefore, when God told mankind they would die if they ate of the forbidden tree, He had to perform it. Clearly God did not want man to die or He would not have warned them. So God's love for man was strong yet He had to allow them to die. This is actually a good thing. Why? Because it demonstrates the Lord's faithfulness! 2 Timothy 2:13 says "If we are unfaithful, he remains faithful, for he cannot deny who he is." In other words, for man to be faithful he must follow the Lord's decrees. However, for the Lord to be faithful, He must follow His own decrees. If God goes against His own words then it would be like disrespecting Himself.

Let's consider a biblical example. Read Matthew 14:1-11. King Herod, ruler of Galilee, had his daughter dance for him at his birthday party. He loved it so much that he promised to give her whatever she wanted. Herodias tells her daughter to request John the Baptist's head on a tray. Upon the daughter's request, Herod regretted his promise but chose to honor the vow. The vow was made in public and so Herod did not want to be seen breaking a vow in front of the guests. So he put out the order for John's head.

I only use this as an example concerning a king's decrees and his faithfulness to them. But Herod was not a godly king! I am not comparing Herod's character to the Creator's. But in comparison to Herod's regret, God did not want Adam and Eve to die. But they did not follow instructions which would have prevented such a punishment. Basically, Adam and Eve committed treason against the kingdom of God. That unlawful act was punishable by death (among other curses).

So Adam and Eve fell into sin. They were naked, ashamed, and afraid. So something had happened to their body and mind because of their sinful action. However, the Lord observed something in Genesis 3:22. God knew that if man was allowed to stay in the garden then they would keep eating from the tree of life and still live forever. God had already promised them that death would follow their disobedience; therefore, He knew what He had to do. In verse 23 Adam and Eve were banished from the garden (which could still provide them eternal life) to cultivate the ground elsewhere.

When one notices the reason why God kicked man out of the garden then a mystery is revealed. The environment in which the garden was consumed by was an environment in which death was impossible. In order to die, man had to leave. Things like sickness, starvation, lack of any kind, natural disasters, disease, loneliness, ignorance, and disabilities were all impossibilities within this environment. The Garden of Eden can be best described as the kingdom of God or the government of God. Isaiah 9:6-7 will give us further insight: "For a child is born to us, a son is given to us. The government will rest on his shoulders. And he will be called: Wonderful Counselor,

THE GOSPEL: THE KINGDOM OF GOD

Mighty God, Everlasting Father, and Prince of Peace. His government and its peace will never end. He will rule with fairness and justice from the throne of his ancestor David for all eternity. The passionate commitment of the LORD of heaven's Armies will make this happen!"

We can see here that a human child is born, a Son from heaven is given, and at least one of His main agendas was to bring a government with Him from heaven. Not only will this Son, Jesus, bring the government, but it will rest on His shoulders. This is because Christ is the foundation of this government. This government, which contain the attributes of peace, fairness, and justice, will never end. Then the Lord's armies are mentioned, which are actually His angels and can defeat any other force (whether human or spiritual) that pits itself against God and His government. Therefore, we can see that God has His military and it is not the people of God. It is His angels. More on this later.

Adam and Eve lost that which they needed most, the kingdom of God. They did not lose God. He is technically everywhere, although the intimate relationship had been severely damaged. The kingdom of God, which is ran and maintained by God Himself, contains all of man's needed provisions. This includes physical, security, social, self-actualization (purpose & destiny), and self-esteem (recognition & power). This is what ultimately killed them, even though God did not want them to die. Indeed man is His most prized creation. So He had to make a way to restore man back to Himself. Let me put it this way. If you tell your child not to climb that tree or else they will get hurt but they climb and get hurt anyway then what are you to do? Would you just stare at them and say "I told you so"? Of course not! You would then provide the solution to their demise. After all, you are their parent, the one who loves them more than any other human does, and their provider. So, you must nurse them back to health even though the consequences they face are deserved due to their disobedience. This is what God did for us!

Court Proceedings:

The Lord had a plan. But first, man (and the serpent) had to be put through an arraignment process by the Judge. What is an arraignment? It is a court process where a criminal defendant is given the charges against him and he has a chance to plead guilty or not guilty. An attorney is provided if they don't have one. Sentencing can happen during the arraignment if the defendant pleads guilty. Adam did plead guilty. The Lord asked Adam if he did the crime in Genesis 3:11. Adam made an excuse but never denied the charge which is as good as stating guilt. The Lord did the same with Eve who responded in the same way that Adam did. Because of the guilty plea, God could immediately come down with the sentencing. Eve was sentenced to pain in child birth and the desire to control her husband who would rule over her. Adam was sentenced with a hard ground to cultivate. No matter how hard he would try, life would be rough from here on out. But before man's curses were stated, they were given the hope of an attorney yet to be revealed. God also cursed the serpent when He said that the woman's offspring would strike his head. This was a foreshadowing of the advocate or lawyer to come. 1 John 2:1 says: "My dear children, I am writing this to you so that you will not sin. But if anyone does sin, we have an advocate who pleads our case before the Father. He is Jesus Christ, the one who is truly righteous." Christ pleads our case in heaven to this very day!

Righteousness:

1 John 2:1 tells us that Christ is the one who is truly righteous. This is an important concept. There are many scriptures discussing righteousness in the Bible but let's go back to one of our keynote scriptures seen in Matthew 6:33: "But seek first the kingdom of God and his righteousness, and all these things will be added to you." So, we have two things to seek here; the kingdom of God and, His righteousness. What is righteousness or what does it mean to be righteous?

Most people think that righteousness is a religious term. It is not. It is actually a legal term. It simply means to be law-abiding, justified, acceptable, blameless, honorable, or excusable. For instance, I myself am not wanted by my local or federal government for any crimes or tax evasion and there is no one to accuse me of such. Therefore, as I write this today,

I am righteous with the government local and at large. Let me put it another way. If someone is accused and convicted of theft then they will go to prison and serve their predetermined time. At this point they are no longer righteous with the government. Indeed, they have a debt to pay. Once their time in prison has come to an end their debt is paid. So, theoretically, once the debt is paid and they are set free then they are righteous, or right aligned with, the government again. At this point, theoretically, they leave prison and are set free to live as if nothing had ever happened. So righteousness refers to one's standing with his or her government.

How can someone become righteous in the kingdom of God? The answer is sobering. They must be perfect! There lies the problem, man is not perfect. Romans 3:10 says: "No one is righteous—not even one." Remember that Matthew 6:33 tells us to seek "His righteousness," not our own perceived righteousness. Therefore, Jesus gives us our righteousness, or right standing, with the government of heaven because of His perfection and position in heaven. This is my point, as written in Philippians 3:9: "...I no longer count on my own righteousness through obeying the law; rather, I become righteous through faith in Christ. For God's way of making us right with himself depends on faith." There it is! Jesus literally gives us His own righteousness to use in becoming perfect in the spirit and, therefore, acceptable to God who is in heaven. Our flesh remains flawed in sin and cursed towards death, "But if through the power of the Spirit you put to death the deeds of your sinful nature, you will live." (Romans 8:13).

The Plan:

What does all of this mean? The serpent was given a promise that the woman would have a child that would crush his head. We know that a child was born that would restore the government of God or, the kingdom of God, back to mankind and therefore restoring man back to God. How does one receive entrance or citizenship into this kingdom? There is only one way in! Jesus spoke of Himself in John 14:6 when He said, "I am the way, the truth, and the life. No one comes to the Father except through Me." You should read the entire chapter to get the full gist of what Jesus is saying here. Jesus spoke of His Father's house which is in heaven. The only way to receive heaven and its government is through Christ. But remember what Jesus prayed in Matthew 6:10: "Your kingdom come. Your will be done on earth as it is in heaven."

God's plan was to bring Himself down in human form to restore mankind to Himself and the kingdom. He would do this by making man righteous with His government again. Jesus died on the cross and paid our death sentence. I will explain the mechanics of this further later on but because of who Christ is, and what He accomplished on the cross, we can return to God unscathed. In other words, we have been redeemed, bought back, from Satan by Christ for God the Father and His kingdom. Now that is Good News! Amen!

The Gospel:

What is the kingdom of God? It is God's government, ways, thoughts, laws, processes, and other attributes which originate in heaven but, are manifested on earth by Christ and through the people of God or, the citizens of the kingdom of God. To enter into this kingdom, one must pledge allegiance to the king whose name is Jesus.

By pledging allegiance, you agree to repent or turn away from, your old way of life, beliefs, and actions. Furthermore, you agree to love Him above all else, submit to His ways, and commune with Him and acknowledge Him in all your ways through reading His word and prayer. The kingdom of God contains everything you need in life including, but not limited to, the Creator of the universe, the King of the earth, love, provision, purpose, destiny, health, wisdom, and any other support needed. A citizen has been given free access to petition heaven for whatever reason is imaginable, with a promise to be answered by God Himself. God's army, His angels, are used to wage war on behalf of the citizens while they reside in safety. This army can also provide protection for you as you come and go whether at home or on the road.

We know we are citizens of this kingdom by the Holy Spirit by which, among other things, gives us confidence of salvation (Romans 8:9, 16). The Holy Spirit also provides our direct link to heaven and is how God provides us with wisdom, directions, revelations, and other things.

We lost the kingdom of God in the Garden of Eden through treason but, it is available again through Jesus Christ if you accept Him as Lord and Savior of your life. To know the Creator of the universe is unfathomable! For this Creator to love us no matter what is unimaginable! Glory to God! Jude 24-25 says it best: "Now to Him who is able to keep you from stumbling, and to present you faultless before the presence of His glory with exceeding joy, to God our Savior, who alone is wise, be glory and majesty, dominion and power, both now and forever. Amen."

PRAYER

Many people struggle with prayer. Most Christians know they are supposed to do it but either fail to pray or, do not do it enough. Many churches hold prayer meetings during the week that go largely unattended. So what is the problem? Could it be our understanding? Prayer is very easy to understand once we focus on its privileges instead of its workload.

I struggled with prayer at the beginning of my adult walk with Christ. I had a few issues. I already believed God to be sovereign. To say that God is sovereign is to express that He has supreme and absolute authority. In other words, His power is checked by no one else in creation. Many scriptures attest to this. 1 Chronicles 29:11-12 describes it thoroughly: "Yours, O Lord, is the greatness, the power, the glory, the victory, and the majesty. Everything in the heavens and on earth is yours, O Lord, and this is your kingdom. We adore you as the one who is over all things. Wealth and honor come from you alone, for you rule over everything. Power and might are in your hand, and at your discretion people are made great and given strength."

The passage speaks of His power and dominion over heaven, earth, and every person who lives. Psalms 115:3 says it best: "Our God is in the heavens, and He does as he wishes." God can and will do whatever He wants to do. So why should I or anyone else try to influence Him through prayer? For instance, I could pray to the Lord to receive a wife. But if I am not ready to love, cherish, and provide for one then He will not give me one because He is concerned for my wife to be. Many times people perceive these kinds of situations to be unanswered prayer. Actually, no prayer goes unanswered.

It is simply up to God whether He will grant them or not. In fact, God has blessed me with things that I know came from Him that I didn't even pray for. So why waste time with prayer, right? I decided that I trusted God to do whatever He wanted in my life. I trusted Him therefore, there was no need to pray much. Simply put, no matter what I pray, God will do what he wants to regardless of my requests.

Another issue I had with prayer came from Matthew 6:8: "your Father knows exactly what you need even before you ask him!" WHAT! Then why am I having to ask the Lord for what I need? He already knows! I can just trust Him for what I need and accept what I get or don't get. Right? Yet the Bible tells us to pray. Once you believe what the Bible says then it is easy to realize that our thoughts are to be perfected by its teachings. So reading the Bible is how we discover that our view of things do not match God's view which is perfect.

The promises of God were another stumbling block for me. He has given us too many to discuss here but I'll name a few. Philippians 4:19 is a favorite among almost all Christians: "And this same God who takes care of me will supply all your needs from his glorious riches, which have been given to us in Christ Jesus." Another favorite is Romans 8:28 which says, "And we know that God causes everything to work together for the good of those who love God and are called according to his purpose for them." The last favorite that I'll mention is Hebrews 13:5. Here Jesus quotes a passage from the Old Testament (Joshua 1:5). Jesus says, "Don't love money; be satisfied with what you have. For God has said, 'I will never fail you. I will never abandon you.'"

There is much to discuss about each one of these passages. However, the only point that I wanted to make was that God has promised to take care of us. Many more scriptures prove this point. Study Matthew chapter 6 when you get a chance. Jesus explains why we shouldn't worry about life because our Heavenly Father will provide the things that we need. I believe all of these promises now and I have for a long time. So you tell me why should we pray? I do not believe that I am the only one asking this question. Apparently believers have not been given enough of a reason to pray as they should.

Maybe the biggest reason people do not pray often is the fact that they cannot see who they are talking to. In addition, God usually does not respond in the same way a parent or friend would respond during a conversation. The thought has crossed my mind many times that I am just talking to myself. Because of this, I often end my prayers with something like, "God, I know you can hear me praying. Thanks for listening." But still, faith is a major factor in one's ability to pray due to the lack of natural and immediate feedback.

Reasons for Prayer:

We have covered the reasons that prayer may not be necessary. Let's discuss the many reasons that we should indeed pray. First, we are commanded to pray. God tells us to make our requests known to Him (Philippians 4:6). Second, we can read in the history of Jesus' life that He prayed often. If the Messiah of the world, the God Man, the sinless Jesus, and the resurrected Lord needed to pray when He was living on this planet, then I think we all need to so much more. Do you agree? We can make sense of it later. Third, God says that He will give us what we ask for (1 John 5:14-15). Jesus says it Himself in Matthew 7:7. He compares praying to a knock on a door. When we do so, there is an expectation for our knock to get an answer.

God promises there will be an answer to our prayers. Actually, we are told that we don't get what we want because we don't ask for it (James 4:2). Fourth, we are told to never stop praying no matter the circumstance or tribulation (1 Thessalonians 5:17). Fifth, prayer can increase and exercise the level of faith that we have at that particular time. Answered prayer increases our faith. The action of praying can as well.

The Bible says that the Holy Spirit pleads for us when we don't know what to pray. That connection between the God in heaven and the God in us can be felt by our natural bodies! You will have to try it to believe it. You can touch heaven during prayer and know that there IS a Creator in the highest heaven who knows you, sees you, is listening to you, loves you, and will never leave you alone! Praise God for that!

Obviously there are a lot of reasons to pray. There are certainly way more reasons than just five. However, there are plenty enough listed to get us going. One can understand and make sense of it later. But do not wait! Pray today, tonight, or right now. Your Father in heaven is waiting on you. He wants a relationship with you. There can never be any relationship with anyone without communication. People even talk to their pets and by doing so begin to see them as a member of the family. Do you say that you are a son or daughter of God? If your answer is yes then prove it! Commune with your Lord.

You may be saying, "But I don't know how to pray." The answer might shock you but prayer is very easy to do. The one thing we need to avoid is the temptation to copy someone else's praying style, how they sound, or maybe even the words that they use. None of this is necessary. What a waste of time it is to try and be someone you are not! Be yourself. You may not like you, but God loves you! Come to Him just as you are today. What am I saying? Let me define prayer for you first. Prayer is simply the act of talking to God. That's it. Nothing more and nothing less. So how do you talk to God? You use the same language, style, accent, volume, articulation, pitch, and any other component of speech of which I am unaware. All you have to do is use the same voice that everyone you come in contact with hears on a regular basis. In other words, your current communication style will work just fine.

All you have to do is talk to God. You can get down on your knees or stand up while you are praying. You can lay down on your back or your stomach. You can hold your hands in praying position or leave them in your pants pockets. You can pray while you wash the dishes or you can find a quiet place. You can close your eyes or leave them open. God will hear your prayer regardless of how you deliver it.

Now listen! We know that God is the King of the universe so I should not have to tell you to approach Him with respect. Respect is to hold someone in high regard, esteem, reverence, admiration, or honor. So how should you respect the Creator of the universe? He is the one who formed everything that is from His thoughts. He is more powerful than all the powers in the universe all put together. He is the only one who was never created. Therefore, He always has been and always will be. His presence is everywhere at all times as He resides in heaven. He has literally counted every single hair on your head. Gravity cannot hold Him down any more than the lack of gravity can pull Him up. He is the creator of all things big and small. Keep that in mind while you are talking to Him. How much should you respect this Guy? That's right…a lot! The ultimate disrespect to God is to ignore Him. He would rather you show your anger towards Him than to act as if He is not even there. Just talk to God!

Perhaps another reason people do not pray is they do not experience enough "answered" prayers. The reason I put the word "answered" in quotes is because when most people talk about answered prayers they are referring to requests made to God that were granted in a way that were desirable. However, technically speaking, all prayers to God are answered. Let's look at it this way. When you call God (pray)…He picks up the phone (answers)…and listens. How He responds is irrelevant to the fact that He answered the call. This is a very important point. We must have faith that God hears our prayers and wants and knows what is best for our life. How He responds is His sovereign choice.

It is necessary to say that God is not a genie in a bottle. He is not available to fulfill our every wish and want. He does not want us to have a craving for everything we see or to have pride in our possessions and accomplishments. A life of physical pleasure alone would cause us to love the many awesome aspects of creation instead of the Creator who created them.

The good news of the kingdom of God is not about a happy life. Spoiler alert! It is about a joyous life.

To have a happy life it is necessary to get most everything you want or desire. When you get what you want then you are happy. When you don't get what you want then you are not happy. Maybe you received adequate transportation but not the exact car you wanted. Maybe God gave you a loving spouse who is not as tall as you would like. Or, maybe you wanted a tailor made suit but could only afford the one on the discount rack. I know these sound like frivolous examples but cases like those listed above govern our happiness in life. Sometimes we get what we want and sometimes we don't. So our happiness is like a roller coaster. Some people cannot seem to get anything to go their way. These people are almost never happy.

In contrast, joy is not dependent on things and circumstances that are outside of our control. Therefore, it is possible to have joy during times of trouble or turmoil (Hebrews 12:2). Joy is strongly connected to hope (Romans 15:13), strength (Nehemiah 8:10), salvation (1 Peter 1:8-9), and is listed as one of the evidences that one indeed has the Holy Spirit working in and through them (Galatians 5:22). Happiness is good but seek after joy! God knows what you need more than you do. If you allow Him to be your sole provider then, even though darkness has befallen you, your joy will come in the morning (Psalm 30:5). That's good news! You don't need better things, circumstances, parents, etc. What you need is the kingdom of

God in your life. Then anything else noteworthy will be given to you if God says it's good for your individual and specific life.

God is not a wishing well. Yet scripture does tell us to have faith and believe that we will get from God what we ask for as is stated in Mark 11:24. However, there are several conditions of the heart that can either aide or restrict God's ability to grant your prayers. In other words, our heart's condition can make it difficult for the Lord to answer our prayers which can result in a delay or, complete prevention for any of them being granted. The Lord wants to and will grant our prayers if we allow Him to do it. You should make a note of these conditions for future reference.

Selfish Motives. A genie in a bottle may grant your selfish desires but the Lord will not. Psalm 37:4 tells us to, "Take delight in the Lord, and He will give you your heart's desires." This is one of the most popular scriptures in the Bible for people to memorize. It's also one of the most misunderstood and misinterpreted scriptures in the Bible. Within this chapter of Psalm, the writer is telling us to trust in the Lord and be fully committed to Him. The psalmist wants us to know that we should not worry about our circumstances or our enemies because the Lord will prevail. Psalm 37:4 is not about getting selfish desires. It's about God giving us the desires that He wants us to have, and then giving us what we desire. This is very important. We are so sinful that we end up wanting the wrong things. God wants to give us the desires that He wants us to have and that are okay for us to yearn after. The scripture is about delighting in the Lord or loving Him for who He is. That, in turn, makes us more and more like Him. Then we begin to think and desire the way He does. Then, when we get what we want, it will be like a child receiving just what they asked for on their birthday or Christmas! James 4:3 mentions prayer as it says, "When you ask, you do not receive, because you ask with wrong motives, that you may spend what you get on your pleasures." This point coincides with the next one.

Pray God's will. One day Jesus was praying (Luke 11). One of his disciples must have wanted what Jesus had in His relationship with the Father. The disciple asked Jesus to teach him how to pray. Jesus' answer was about the same as what He said about prayer during His sermon in Matthew 6:9-13 when He said: "Pray like this: Our Father in heaven, may your name be kept holy. May your Kingdom come soon. May your will be done on earth, as it is in heaven. Give us today the food we need, and forgive us our sins as we have forgiven those who sin against us. And don't let us yield to temptation, but rescue us from the evil one." Before I go any further, notice that Jesus said to, "pray like this" not, "pray this." In other words, reciting this prayer is good to do but, that was not what Jesus had in mind. "The Lord's Prayer," as it is affectionately called, shows us the mechanics of how and why to pray. There is much to understand about this prayer from Jesus which is why I discussed it earlier in this book. For now I want us to focus on verse 10 from Matthew 6.

After we address the Father in our prayer (because He is the one we are talking to) then the main point of our prayer is mentioned, whether in literal words or, just in idea or thought. We need to pray for God's kingdom (which includes all of God's provision for our life) to come down to earth and govern the earthly realm in the same way heaven (which is where the Father resides) is governed. Therefore, we should want God's will to be done in our life on the planet earth just like His will is established in heaven. In other words, we should want what God's perfect idea is for life on the earth to happen in the exact same way that He wants it to happen. That is a prayer that God wants to grant.

How do we know what God's will is so we can pray for it? There are things the Bible tells us to pray about. For instance 1 Timothy 2 and 3 tells us to pray for government authorities. We can also follow the example of people who were praying in the Bible. The book of Psalms, for instance, is full of prayers for us to consider. The whole Bible is full of prayers. Romans 8:26-27 tells us that the Holy Spirit helps us when we pray since we often don't know the will of God. The Holy Spirit within us is always in harmony with God's will. Therefore we must lean on the spirit of God when we pray and not our own understanding. Ask for wisdom about what to pray and God will give it to you.

Unconfessed sin. In Psalm 66, the writer is praising God for all that He has done for him. The psalmist exclaims that he had cried out to the Lord for help and He listened. The writer also wrote in verse 18, "If I had not confessed the sin in my heart, the Lord would not have listened." The fact is that sin can form a barrier between us and God. I don't mean that God does not have the power to answer our prayer while we are in sin because He has all power. I don't even mean that God punishes us when we sin by choosing not to listen or grant our prayers. Sin forms a barrier between us and God because God is holy. To commune with Him we must be holy as well. The only way to get this attribute is for Christ to give it to you by your faith in Him.

Once we are holy (through no work of our own), God tells us how to live so that we can maintain our relationship with Him. Comparably to a marriage between a husband and wife. They must agree to be faithful to and not cheat on one another in order to maintain the relationship. When we protect the sin in our life from God (the one who can destroy sin), we are purposely cheating on Him. The barrier that is built is due to the shame of the individual (which makes someone want to distance themselves from God). This is very important.

The other important point here is that we have been given dominion or the right to reign on the earth by the Father Himself. Our right to rule means God will not touch the will we have to rebel against Him. If you sin against God without repentance, what you are telling God is that you do not need the kingdom of God to reside in and govern your life. Therefore, God respects your decision and may choose to leave you to your devices until you choose to turn away from the sin and towards God.

The type of sin that I am referring to here is harbored sin or, wrong doing that we actually protect and try to hide from God. These areas of our life we have not surrendered to the Lord. It is important to know that there is a kingdom of darkness that tries to mimic the kingdom of God. You can read this in Colossians 1:13. Francis Frangipane wrote in his book, *The Three Battlegrounds*, "Satan has a legal access, given to him by God, to dwell in the domain of darkness. Thus, we must grasp this point: The devil can traffic in any area of darkness, even the darkness that still exists in a Christian's heart." Francis is not talking about demon possession in this statement but demonic oppression. This can occur when a person harbors sin in their life. This creates a "safe place" for sin or, as the Bible calls it, a stronghold. One's will to protect the sin in their life will keep God from performing the way He wants to because He would have to override your will. That is why Jesus said in Matthew 3:2, "Repent of your sins and turn to God, for the Kingdom of Heaven is near." Therefore, live a lifestyle of repentance (which does not include plans to do it again) and God will surely hear from heaven and perform works according to your prayers.

Disobedience. The recipe for disobedience is to turn away from scripture. Proverbs 28:9 says, "God detests the prayers of a person who ignores the law." Also 1 John 3:22 says, "And we will receive from him whatever we ask because we obey him and do the things that please him." When we obey the Lord then we will not feel any guilt or shame. Both of these things can form a barrier between us and God. We must give the guilt or shame to God and then, after He erases the guilt or shame from us, He will instruct us on what to remove from our life that caused those barriers in the first place. Sin and disobedience goes hand in hand.

Sin isn't just about doing "bad things". We sin anytime we do not follow the Lord's instructions which we can read in the Bible or those that He gives directly to us via the Holy Spirit. What does this have to do with our prayers being granted? The Lord wants to grant the prayers of His servants. Those who are disobedient do not serve the Lord (at least not in every area). The Lord will always try to steer you back on course. If He grants all of your prayers while you live a life of disobedience then you would have no motivation to turn from your way and towards God. In other words, the Lord uses trials, testing, mishaps, destruction, and pain to get you to reconsider your course of action. When you call on His name then He may simply point you in the right direction rather than give you what you want.

When we obey the Lord we can be confident our prayers will be granted since we're following the Lord's path. Basically, when the Lord tells you to do something, He must provide for it. He is our provider. If you go left when the Lord told you to go right, He is not motivated to make your way work against His way. Make sense? Psalm 37:23 says, "The Lord directs the steps of the godly. He delights in every detail of their lives." In other words, if you allow the Lord to be your road map then He will make sure there are no roadblocks obstructing your journey or He will remove them. Amen!

Unforgiveness. Jesus said in Matthew 6:14-15, "If you forgive those who sin against you, your heavenly Father will forgive you. But if you refuse to forgive others, your Father will not forgive your sins." The key word here is refuse. That word indicates the person understands about forgiveness and its importance but still refuses to do it. Jesus makes it clear what the outcome for that iniquity (invisible sin) will be. The Father will not forgive you! Now remember, we receive forgiveness when we repent and believe in the Lord. A major part of repentance is asking for forgiveness.

If the Lord will not forgive you, then that means He heard your prayer for forgiveness and refused to grant the request! This is very important to understand. If the Lord will not hear your request for forgiveness, which is vital in the kingdom of God since life and death literally hinge upon it, then what other prayers might He ignore? This is worth a lot of consideration.

Jesus says in Mark 11:24-25, "I tell you, you can pray for anything, and if you believe that you've received it, it will be yours. But when you are praying, first forgive anyone you are holding a grudge against, so that your Father in heaven will forgive your sins, too."

Doubt. Doubt is simply a lack of faith. In Matthew 21 we can read about Jesus' journey to Jerusalem. At this time He became hungry and wanted to eat off of a fig tree. But when He approached the tree He saw no figs available to eat, only leaves. So Jesus cursed the fig tree and it immediately withered up and died. The disciples were amazed by this. Jesus took advantage of the moment to teach them about faith. He said in Matthew 21:21: "I tell you the truth, if you have faith and don't doubt, you can do things like this and much more...You can pray for anything, and if you have faith, you will receive it." So, your prayers being granted are contingent upon whether you have faith or not.

What is faith? Hebrews 11:1 defines it for us: "Faith is the confidence that what we hope for will actually happen; it gives us assurance about things we cannot see." In verse 6 we read "And it is impossible to please God without faith." There is a very important principle here. Faith is the "gasoline" that makes the kingdom of God work here on earth. Think about a car. It does not matter how much horsepower it has. Without gasoline it will not work for you. The kingdom of God here on earth is the same way. It must use our faith to function.

We must believe in it even though we can't see it. Just like you believe a car will provide for your transportation, you must also believe the kingdom of God will provide for your life even though you can't see it.

Why won't God grant your prayer when you doubt? When we doubt it simply means that we don't think God can or will perform the work that we are asking for. One day a man came up to Jesus with hopes that He would heal his boy who was possessed by a demon. The man said to Jesus in Mark 9:22, "Have mercy on us and help us, if you can." Jesus quickly responded, "What do you mean, 'if I can'?" Jesus needed to know if the man believed in Him or not because without faith He would not have been able to perform the task. Jesus followed up by saying, "Anything is possible if a person believes." When we believe that our circumstances are greater than God then the circumstance itself becomes like a god to us. If we believe in the "god of circumstance" more than the Creator, then we have chosen it over Him and, once again, God will not touch our will.

The good news is, if we lack faith, then we can pray for some. The father of the boy made a brilliant request of Jesus. He asked, "I do believe, but help me overcome my unbelief!" That request was enough to move Jesus to heal the boy. There are different levels of faith. If you need some more, just ask for it!

Pride. In James 4:6 we can read a Proverb quoted when he writes, "God opposes the proud but favors the humble." How does this relate to prayer? Obviously if you are a proud person and God opposes you that can hinder your prayers. One way we can be proud is to not feel like we need God in every area of our life. Another way to be proud is the urge to look godly rather than being godly. Or maybe you are godly but act a certain way in public so that everyone else knows you are godly. God will not tolerate that kind of heart.

Humble people believe their reward comes from heaven and not people. Jesus was teaching the disciples this sort of thing one day. He explained it further when He mentioned prayer. Jesus instructs in Matthew 6:5-6 for people to not be like hypocrites who love to pray in public places where a crowd can see them. The admiration from others is the only reward Jesus promises those kind of folks. Jesus says a better way is to pray in private where you can't put on a show for others. Surely the Lord will reward you then. Jesus also tells the hearers to not repeat words over and over again in their prayer. These kind of people think God will hear and grant their prayers because they use many words. The pride is in thinking God will answer the prayers due to performance. Just simply approach God with nothing in your hands to give Him except your heart. Then the Lord will reward your humility when He grants your prayers.

Idolatry. We can see in the Bible that idols were (and still can be) figurines made out of stone, wood, gold, silver, or bronze that were labeled as gods whose power only existed in the minds of the people who worshipped them. This is idolatry, and God despises it. Read it for yourself. He makes this abundantly clear in Exodus 20:3-5. Many other places in the Bible confirm this fact. God demands that we worship only Him. John Bevere writes a great explanation of this in his book, *Killing Kryptonite*: "The heart of idolatry is not statues, figurines, altars, or temples. These are only byproducts of a deeper issue. Idolatry is humanity putting aside what God clearly wants in order to satisfy cravings or desires that are contrary to His wishes." John goes on to say "A Christian engages in idolatry when he or she disregards what God has clearly revealed in order to obtain a strong desire…That man or woman has elevated their desire above God's will and formed an idol."

Many times in the Bible, idolatry is compared to adultery (Ephesians 5:21-33; Jeremiah 3:20). A marriage between a man and a woman is basically an agreement to be committed wholly to each other, including not having sex with anyone else. How can a wife who has been unfaithful to her husband then come home and ask or demand faithfulness from him? That doesn't make sense, right? Furthermore, is the husband wrong for wanting or demanding faithfulness from his wife? Of course not! Even Jesus knew He was in the midst of an adulterous generation (Matthew 12:39; 16:4). How can idolatry or spiritual adultery hinder your prayers to God? When we pray to God while harboring idols in our life then, it is like a wife returning home from an extramarital affair and asking her husband for his love, attention, and provision. What an absurd request! Thank God we can repent, turn away from our idols, and receive God's forgiveness. Amen! Just remember this: any good husband, loves to please his faithful wife.

Four more. You should always be asking the Holy Spirit to change you from the inside out. That alone will take care of many of these issues. Don't look at this list as a set of rules, rather a set of guidelines. Communication with God is vital to your life here on the planet earth. We must learn how to do it well. Communication with God will keep you in touch with the government in heaven which can rescue you in times of need. That being said, here are a few more things to consider:

Prayers should be heartfelt and personal. Not robotic. Earnest prayers are powerful and effective. (James 5:16)

P.U.S.H. (pray until something happens). Always pray with persistence. If you are not seeing results then pray some more. Don't give up! Study Luke chapter 11.

Remain in Christ while His words also remain in you. With this being the case, you can ask for whatever you want and it will be granted! (John15:1-7)

Pray in the name of Jesus! This isn't just a phrase we say at the end of our requests to God. It is how we use His authority in our life. (John 14:13-14)

Prayer is easy to do but it should not be taken lightly. What a privilege it is to usher down the kingdom and will of God into our lives and into the lives of others! Prayer can prompt God to overturn the forces of nature (if need be) on your behalf so that you will find success in life. Indeed, nothing is impossible for God! Therefore, nothing is impossible for you. Just think about that for a minute.

Mankind's Dominion

Prayer is a vital component to our life as a believing citizen of the kingdom of God. It must be done. But maybe that's our problem. It's knowing we have to do it. It just seems like work, right? Let me continue to talk about my growth as a praying man. You can see why I thought prayer could not change my life. It seemed to me that if I just believed in the Lord and His promises, then I could rest assured that my provision did not hinge on whether I prayed or not. After all, God is the boss. He will never do something that He does not want to do. He always has my best interest at heart. The Bible clearly lets us know the many reasons why we should pray. One reason we should pray is that we are commanded to. Another is that prayer indeed affects the life of the believer in a positive way. Now remember, I am trying to share my thoughts as they were when I was a young man in Christ. Does anybody feel like they are standing in between the sovereignty of God and their duty to pray?

I am not a religious man. In other words, doing things by repetition based on a sense of duty alone will not get me to comply. I must know the mechanics of a thing. For example, I am not the best rule follower in the world. This may not be the best attribute to have but, it's true for many people. Some say rules are meant to be broken. That is not my belief. I just simply need a good reason as to why the rule is necessary. Almost everyone believes in the rule to not drink and drive. The results could seriously hurt or kill people. The rule is in place to protect the citizens. The same is true for car speed limits. So why do so many people speed? Why is there not an assigned 24 hour task force in every city to stop people from breaking speeding laws? Whatever the actual reality, most people see speeding laws as generalities. So one may think a limit of 55 mph means 55 mph give or take 5-10 mph. Needless to say, we all know people whose speed limit deviation is much higher than 5 or 10 mph. It may be because cars and roads have progressed over the years. Many roads, especially some highways and most interstates, are built for speed. Most think that going 65 mph in a 55 mph zone is not even close to being unsafe. I tend to agree with that. I am not trying to argue as to whether or not certain speed limits should be in place. I am just trying to get you to think about why you, probably, don't obey them to the exact number. Now, back to my past thoughts on praying. I needed a better reason than duty or obligation to pray as much as I should.

Go back and read Genesis 1:26. The scripture says "let them have…" and is a critical statement. God is giving mankind something here. But what is it? God is giving them dominion so mankind can reign and rule here on the planet earth. But what would mankind dominate, rule, or reign over? The scripture says it would be over all the animals on the planet. In verse 28 God says mankind is to govern or subdue the earth. This would include all seed bearing plant life on earth, as we can see in verse 29. God also gave plant life to the animals, in verse 30, but mankind was to dominate the animals. So mankind was given the entire earth to govern or control.

We must not look past or ignore this transaction. God is giving mankind power, or authority, on the planet earth. God would maintain His ultimate, or sovereign, authority yet man was given authority for the planet earth. God's idea was for us to represent heaven on earth. The plan was for man to govern the earth just like God would govern it if He was present in an earthly or natural body. Remember Genesis 1:26: "Let us make human beings in our image, to be like us." So mankind was not to be God or look like God. They were to act like God would and think like God would as His representatives on the planet earth.

The serpent tricked Adam and Eve in the garden by telling them that eating from the forbidden tree would not kill them. The serpent stated that it would make them like God "knowing both good and evil", in Genesis 3:5. Being like God was not a bad thing but they were only supposed to know what God wanted them to know. Evil was not an idea that God wanted man to know or understand.

Mankind was to be God's representatives. Out of all living things on earth, including all plant and wild life, mankind was the only one given authority. Notice that God gave mankind dominion or authority. Part of being in God's image or likeness was the ability to have free choice or autonomy (autonomy is the right to self-government) on the planet earth. The idea of free choice allowed Adam and Eve the ability to disobey God and eat of the forbidden tree. So man had the right, to give their God given authority away to Satan in the garden.

Immediately after the fruit was eaten, Adam and Eve felt shame and nakedness. These two feelings were impossible up to this point in time. Adam and Eve were perfect beings who had nothing to be ashamed of and were oblivious to their nakedness due to God's glory around them. Mankind sinned at the tree and gave their power, authority, and dominion over to an outsider. THIS IS HIGH TREASON UPON THE KING OF THE UNIVERSE! Yet, it was allowed by God. But why? Man had been given the authority to make their own decisions. God's original idea was for mankind to make their own decisions but also to include or acknowledge Him by receiving His wisdom and understanding. Mankind was supposed to hear God's wisdom within His warning to avoid the forbidden tree, take God's wisdom as their own, and operate their earthly government accordingly. In other words, God would give man an idea, man would agree with that idea, and then manifest that idea onto the planet earth. Man would not be forced to do that but, would want to do that due to their love for God the Creator. However, this did not happen because Adam and Eve had something called pride. This feeling was introduced to them by the serpent who was the "father of pride" (refer to Ezekiel 28 and Isaiah 14 for the background story).

Man was the only being given authority on earth by God. Man gave it away to Satan, the serpent in the garden. This is why he is called, "the god of this world" (2 Corinthians 4:4), "the commander of the powers in the unseen world" (Ephesians 2:2), and "the ruler of this world" (John 12:31). In other words, Satan's ideas permeate or spread throughout the earth and it began in the garden. When the Bible mentions "world" it is referring to an arrangement of thoughts or ideas which can therefore be referred to as a government. This world or government the Bible is alluding to is invisible. It is not referencing any earthly government like democracy, socialism, or something else. It is talking about the principalities, powers, rulers of darkness, and spiritual hosts (demons) in the heavenly places (Ephesians 6:12). Every territory on earth is governed by demonic forces that are completely against God the Creator. This doesn't mean that Satan has all power. Yet he does maintain the power that is allowed to him by God. He does not control those who are saved but, he can oppress them. However, he does control all unsaved persons, which make up the vast majority of the planet earth. We know unsaved persons are the majority because we are called a "chosen few" (Matthew 22:14;

Romans 9:27-28). This gives Satan a great amount of influence and authority on the planet earth.

Satan activates his authority through people. He influences those without salvation, and oppresses those who are saved by Christ. Take note of this: Satan needs mankind to agree with his ideas before they will have any influence or power on earth. Remember, the serpent had to talk Adam and Eve into his way of thinking before his ideas could have any power. Satan did not have the power to make Adam and Eve do anything. He still doesn't! Satan persuaded mankind to agree with him and he is still doing that today. Satan has to have people agree with him or he can never have influence on the planet! This is so important to understand! Cain would never have had the ability to even think of killing his brother, Able, if their parents had not allowed Satan's ways of thinking into the earthly realm (Genesis 4). Where did Cain get the idea for murder? It wasn't God!

Satan has to have mankind take on his ideas so he can wield authority on the planet. Satan has been given authority by mankind but it is illegal for him to use it. God established mankind to have authority on earth. So for Satan's authority to become legal, he must get a man or woman to agree with him and activate his ways onto the earth. Satan's far reaching influence comes from all the people of the world who hear his suggestions and agree with him. Satan is the ruler of the unseen world. His rule and influence permeates the earth through all types of media including television, music, movies, books, signs, and people. If every person on the planet would turn to God for salvation, all at the same time, then Satan would have zero authority, command, or influence on the earth.

God has sovereign authority in the universe. Technically He can do whatever He wants, whenever He wants. But, He gave mankind dominion or authority, which is the ability to reign on the earth. God wanted to give man ideas so they would agree with those ideas, and then would activate those ideas onto the planet. So if mankind does not agree with God's ideas, then God would have to overthrow man's power and authority, which He has the right and ability to do, in order to activate His ideas. This would establish His authority on the planet. God will not do that, though. But why?

When God said "let them" in Genesis 1:26, He gave His word to man. Remember the story of King Herod? He regretted the promise given to his daughter that she could have anything, up to half the kingdom if she desired (Mark 6:14-29). Herod, who was not a just or godly man, would not overturn his publicly stated promise in order to refuse the beheading of John the Baptist. God, who is righteous to judge all, and is perfect in all of His ways, will not overturn His word either. If God did, then His words would be meaningless and powerless. Mankind would never be able to trust Him. God is always faithful to His word. Herod isn't fit to be compared to God but, if Herod would be faithful to his word as king, then you know God has been, and always will be faithful to His word.

God gave man dominion in the garden and, in spite of man's transgressions, has remained faithful to His words. This explains why God did not step in and stop man from sinning before it was too late. God knows everything and knew what was going on but allowed it to take place. Man had been given the authority to do what they did even though it was wrong. Part of being in God's image is the autonomy to self-govern. So God must find people who hear His words, agree with His words, and activate or manifest His words onto the planet earth. God always has a remnant of people willing to do just that at all times all around the planet (1 Kings 19:14-18). God can do whatever He wants to do and is powerful enough to do as He pleases (Psalm 115:3) but, He will not ever be unfaithful to His word towards mankind. Therefore, mankind is the only being with legal right to authority on the planet.

To have legal authority on the planet one must be a human which means having an earthly body. Satan does not have an earthly body so he must find someone who does and influence them to carry out his ideas and thoughts. He is very good at this. Ultimately, Satan would love to have one of his demons possess a man or woman so they can have almost complete control of their body. Why else would demonic forces be interested in human possession? Total access to a human body is even more authority and dominion on the earth.

Likewise, the Lord is trying to inhabit a human body with His Holy Spirit. Please understand this! The Lord wants to inhabit a human body with His spirit so He can use their body to establish His will on the planet earth. This explains why Jesus stated in Luke 15:7: "I say to you that likewise there will be more joy in heaven over one sinner who repents than over ninety-nine just persons who need no repentance." Every time a sinner repents and turns to God then a new human body has been added to the Lords legion which expands His reach of influence on the planet. That means one more person to agree with Him, obey or do as He instructs, and recruit more followers. Follow me closely here! If God wants to heal a person of cancer then He can pick one citizen of His kingdom to lay hands on them, believe, and pray for it to happen. The person being used is powerless to reverse such a disease as cancer. Yet the person is able to siphon or appropriate God's power from heaven to be used for healing. This is possible due to the person's salvation, or registry into citizenship, of the kingdom of God and their faith in God's faithfulness and power.

Earthly Interference:

Let's look at it another way. If God wants to heal someone of cancer then He needs a man or woman on earth to agree with that idea. This man or woman would have to agree with an idea that is invisible or has not been manifested yet. This kind of agreement is called faith! "Faith is the confidence that what we hope for will actually happen; it gives us assurance about things we cannot see" (Hebrews 11:1). So a man or woman would have to agree, or believe, that God wants this person healed of cancer and has already done it in heaven. The healing simply needs to be manifested on earth just like it is in heaven. Sound familiar? It's no wonder Jesus wants us to pray, "May your will be done on earth, as it is in heaven" (Matthew 6:10). So a human being who believes that a cancer patient has already been healed in heaven, prays for the person, so healing can be manifested on earth.

Man was given dominion in the Garden of Eden. Along with this dominion is God's permission to self-govern. Man used this permission to usher sin into the earth. Now all kinds of things are a part of the earth experience that was not originally supposed to be, including disease. Yes, cancer is a byproduct of sin on the earth (along with natural disasters, sickness, death, etc.). In other words, cancer, for instance, is the fault of the human being. Cancer is not God's fault! Cancer on the earth is a product of man's abused dominion. So how do we get cancer to leave a person? WE HAVE TO ASK THE LORD TO INTEFERE, OR INTERUPT, OUR DOMINION! Mankind has been given dominion and authority on earth by God. But a man or woman of the Most High God wants God's dominion and authority instead of their own (Matthew 6:10). This is because mankind's dominion and authority created the cancer by allowing sin but is not powerful enough to control or kill it.

Mankind must ask God to interfere or cancel out their authority in a given situation or a particular instance. Man has to relinquish his authority and give God permission to establish His authority. I hope you are getting this! Considering our scenario, if God wants a person healed of cancer then He must find a human being who will agree with His idea and cause it to manifest on earth through their faith in God by prayer. God cannot heal a person of cancer if there is no human being who will agree with it! Prayer is more than just talking to God. Prayer is a transaction between God and man where man gives up his authority and dominion, at a given time and in a given situation, and asks God to bring His will, authority, and dominion out of heaven and establish it into the earthly realm.

I know this may be hard to grasp or understand, but this is how the Lord has always operated. Study Exodus in the Bible. In chapter 3 & 4 we see that God had a will in heaven to free the people of Israel from Egypt because He heard their cries for help. God needed to attract a man to agree with this idea, and help God establish it from heaven and onto earth. So God burned a bush to attract Moses and hire him for the job. Moses didn't want to do it which caused God to make concessions towards him, like providing Aaron to help him speak, and showing him a miracle with the staff and cloak. Fast forward to Exodus 7:1, God told Moses "I will make you seem like God to Pharaoh." Remember, mankind is to be the "moon" to God's "sun" by using His light as their own. Down to Exodus 7:17, God wanted to turn the Nile into blood so, He had Moses announce it and have the water struck with a staff. Moses and Aaron have no power of their own here. The staff has no power here either. God needed man to agree with His idea (faith), announce His idea on the earth (prayer), and then activate their faith through some sort of action (obedience). Then God's will in heaven, to have the Nile turn to blood, actually happened on earth. God needed Moses to play his part. God could have done all of this on His own but He needed man to agree because He gave man dominion on the planet earth.

Are you yet convinced? Study 1 Kings 18. Elijah was told to announce to king Ahab that rain would be coming soon. Elijah agreed with God's idea to send rain which took a lot of faith since there had not been any rain in that region for three years! Secondly, Elijah obeyed God by actually telling Ahab this would happen (verse 41) before there were any physical signs to support such a claim. Then Elijah prayed (verse 42) for the rain to come. But why did God need Elijah in order to make this happen? Elijah had a human body which meant he had authority and dominion on earth. Elijah agreed with the Lord's idea for rain, obeyed God's command to tell Ahab, and then prayed for God's will, which was in heaven, to establish itself on earth. This produced a very large rain storm. This is how it works, folks!

Need more proof? Read Acts 14. Paul came upon a crippled man who had never walked before. Paul realized the man had the faith to be healed just by looking at him. This is called discernment. That is when God reveals to a person a previously kept secret in heaven. In verse 10, Paul told the man to stand up, which was impossible! Basically, God wanted to heal the man, Paul agreed, and then announced God's plan by faith.

God has always used mankind to get work done on the earth. Check out Genesis 2:19-20. Why do you think God gave Adam the task of naming all the animals? Adam had a human body and the authority in order to do the job.

The Bible is full of examples of mankind's authority. How about this? Go and try to find where the Lord wants to act in some way on the earth and does not use a human in any way, shape, or form. Read about Noah (Genesis 6-8). God wanted to flood the earth but needed a human to agree and build a boat so humanity could be preserved. Read about how the Lord wanted to destroy Sodom and Gomorrah (Genesis 18). The Lord had a plan but first wanted to confide in Abram (Abraham) before He acted out His plan. Abram agreed with the plan but wanted any righteous people to be spared. Abram's request was granted.

Maybe you will understand the power and purpose of prayer after you read Matthew 16:19. Jesus said to His disciples, "And I will give you the keys of the Kingdom of Heaven. Whatever you forbid on earth will be forbidden in heaven, and whatever you permit on earth will be permitted in heaven." This is how God's heavenly government works! Through prayer mankind forbids or permits things on earth. So, to pray for healing is to forbid sickness on earth. Then God brings His will for healing (James 5:14-15) out of heaven and into the earthly situation. If you are lacking basic necessities like shelter, clothing, or food then you need to pray and loose God's provision in your life. That is permitting prosperity in your life through prayer. Then God brings His will for your provision (Philippians 4:19) out of heaven and into your life here on earth. Why do we have to pray? Because the universe is messed up due to our sin but, through faith in Jesus, we can still get heaven on earth, if we just believe!

God needs humans with earthly bodies who have dominion on earth to agree with Him and allow Him to step in and override their authority so He can establish His own authority. God and Satan want the same thing: human bodies. I know this sounds like the 1978 film "Invasion of the Body Snatchers" but, what I am talking about is the real thing. God nor Satan will force you to do anything. However both need your influence on the earth in order to exercise their will or plans. If you are still on the fence concerning all of this, I have one more piece of evidence that will close my case.

Let's go back to Genesis 3. Mankind had sinned at the forbidden tree and was now sentenced to die. God wanted to save them but He had no legal access to the earthly realm (due to His own arrangement). Satan needed to be defeated by someone with a human body who had legal dominion and authority on earth. Mankind could not do it since they had fallen into sin, sentenced to death, and no longer perfect. So God had to save man, right? But God didn't have a body. However, God did have a plan! The Lord began to curse the serpent in verse 14. First, the serpent was cursed to crawl on its belly. Next, God created hostility between the serpent and the woman. Then, God created hostility between the serpent and her offspring. God said in verse 15, referring to her offspring, "He will strike your head, and you will strike his heel." The offspring that God is alluding to would one day be called Immanuel, the Christ, Jesus! Don't you see? God needed a body to have legal authority on earth and save mankind from their demise. So He planned to put his Spirit into a human body. That way He could be fully God and fully man at the same time. The plan was to take back what Satan had bargained away from mankind. God could not do it immediately. He needed a body.

Jesus was a man who had a body and the dominion that went with it. But also He was God, perfect and in righteous position with the Father, to restore man back to God and the kingdom of God back to man. God couldn't stop man from sinning at the forbidden tree because He didn't have a human body which would have given Him legal right to negotiate at the tree. But, through Jesus who is the Christ, God had power AND dominion. Now that same power Jesus used while on earth, we can use in our life on earth, through the Holy Spirit.

We use prayer to commune and form a relationship with God. But when we need to get things done and need supernatural interference within our earthly realm, we call on God. We relinquish our dominion and authority, at a given time and in a given situation, and watch the Lord move miraculously within our situation. He can do things that we cannot. God can fix a marriage, calm a storm, protect your children, send you money, heal your body, give you wisdom, mend a hurting heart, cure an addiction, or anything else you need while on this planet. We are not alone! God is for us if we keep our faith in Him. There may not be a way out of your situation, but God will make a way. Just call His will down from heaven. All you need is a human body, a relationship with the Lord, and some faith. Pray to God and all things will be possible!

WHO IS GOD

The word "god" is a generic term. So Christians have taken to capitalizing the "G" in the word so as to make their god stand out above the rest. Even the Bible suggests that there are many gods. However, there are only many gods due to the perception and perspective of mankind. In other words, mankind has ascribed divine or godly status to many people, animals, or things that do not deserve such reverence. Some might say that Satan or angels are gods due to their ability to transcend nature. Indeed, no human on earth could ever kill or subdue Satan or an angel. So does that make them a god? Some people think that humans are gods and actually try to use biblical scripture to support that claim. They refer to Psalm 82:6 and John 10:34 which both describe mankind as a god. However, upon reading the texts in their entirety, one can see that the Bible does not agree with the thought of mankind being divine. But, mankind was created in the image of God, and is supposed to represent God here on earth in everything that they do. In that way, mankind would then seem like a god while, in actuality, only mimicking or embodying the image of God.

In Exodus 7:1 for instance, God caused Moses to "be like God," or "seem like God," to Pharaoh. Moses was not actually a god by himself. In contrast, the serpent in the Garden of Eden succeeded in tricking Eve into eating of the forbidden tree (Genesis 3:5) by telling her she would become, "like God." This was a lie. The only way that she could be like God or embody His image would be for her to obey God. Therefore, when she ate of the tree that God commanded her not to eat from, she ceased to be like God. We can only mimic God's nature by obeying His commandments. Indeed, Adam and Eve were never gods but had the job of representing God on earth. They were to do and say things the way God would if He were physically on the planet.

Paul, our beloved apostle, says it best in 1 Corinthians 8:5-6: "There may be so-called gods both in heaven and on earth, and some people actually worship many gods and many lords. But we know that there is only one God, the Father, who created everything, and we live for him. And there is only one Lord, Jesus Christ, through whom God made everything and through whom we have been given life." We are to believe, as Paul did, that there is only one true God. This integral, fundamental, and inherent truth or teaching of our faith is explicitly stated in scripture many times. Isaiah 46:9 is one of many where God Himself states: "For I alone am God! I am God, and there is none like me." Therefore, it is important to know that our faith is in one God and only one God! This is a theme that can be found in the Bible from beginning to end. His name is Jehovah or Yahweh (Lord), El Shaddai (Lord God Almighty), El Elyon (The Most High God), Elohim (God), Adonai (Lord), and others. But who is God?

Man has been given the ability to know God as far as He has revealed Himself to us. Before we go any further in our discussion of God, it is important to know that we can never fully understand God. This is because God is immeasurable (Psalm 145:3), incomprehensible (Psalm 147:5), and beyond our thoughts and ways (Isaiah 55:8-9). We can know God, but not in the exhaustive sense. However, everything we do know about God is very true. It is true that God is spirit (John 4:24), God is fair and just (Romans 3:26), God is light (1 John 1:5), and God is love (1 John 4:8). These are all things that we know about God even if we cannot fully understand these and other attributes ascribed to Him in the Bible. We can know facts about God in how He acts or thinks. We can also know God on a personal level like one would to a friend or family member. That is not to say that we can know everything there is to know about God. Yet He is our Father (Romans 8:15) and friend (James 2:23). The terms "father" and "friend" denotes a very close and personal relationship between two people. One must know another before such a bond can be formed but we can never truly know 100% of a person and that fact is much truer concerning God.

Let's take a very brief survey on the many attributes or characteristics of God. This is not an exhaustive list but it will get us started in knowing the answer to the question, "Who is God?"

GOD IS INDEPENDENT (Acts 17:24-25). Why did God decide to create humanity? Is was not because He was lonely. In fact, God does not need anything in creation. The only thing that God needs is Himself. He does not get bored nor is He incapable of handling things on His own. God was never created. Therefore, He does not have a beginning or an end. If God ever needed anyone or anything then He would cease being who He is, which is impossible. God wants a relationship with you and me but, He does not need one. God wants you to obey and do His will on earth but if you don't then He will find some other way to usher in His will. God wants you to work for Him more than you will ever know or be able to quantify. Yet God does not need you at all.

GOD IS UNCHANGEABLE (Psalm 102:25-27). Who God is or His character has never and will never change. God cannot get worse or better. He has always been the same way He is today and will be tomorrow. God does feel emotion though. Some people think that the God of the Old Testament is different from the God of the New Testament. Indeed, God shows His anger most often in the Old Testament scripture. However, in the New Testament, since Jesus has bestowed grace upon us, God is withholding the effects of His anger for a period of time. It is not that God does not get angry. He is withholding the passion of His anger until an appointed time of judgement. Mankind can love someone one day and then hate them the next. God does not do that. He loves mankind but hates sin and He can do both at the same time. In the Old Testament, we can see God's judgement on mankind. This is not just an activity of His anger. God's love and anger function at the same time. There are places in the Bible where God is seen changing His mind (Jonah 3:10) but that only happens when people repent of their ways and change. So, God acts differently according to the situation but He does not change in His being or ultimate purposes. If God is unchangeable in His attributes of justice and mercy then He must respond differently when people act differently. Otherwise, how people act would be meaningless to God. Therefore, He would not be the just and merciful God we can read about in the Bible.

GOD IS ETERNAL (Deuteronomy 33:27). God has no beginning and no end. That is why He is called the Alpha and Omega, which are the first and last letters in the Greek alphabet respectively. So God starts and ends everything but, He has no starting or ending point. God created time but He is not governed by time like we are. God sees the past, present, and future all at the same time. God is timeless. That does not mean that He does not deal with time accordingly. That is why

God can deal with people differently when they repent even though He knew they would repent all along. God is far away in heaven and eternity. Yet He can sit right next to you in time and deal with just that moment in your life. Peter said, "A day is like a thousand years to the Lord, and a thousand years is like a day" (2 Peter 3:8). Many people try to use this as a measuring stick to figure out certain mysterious time frames in the Bible. But, those people are wasting their time. This quote just means that God is not governed by time at all. God can deal with mankind in time seemingly without regard to what He knows will happen in the future. Everything God does, embodies the perspective of eternity.

GOD IS OMNIPRESENT (Jeremiah 23:23-24). Omnipresent literally means "all present." God is everywhere, all at the same time, and is not bound by space. He cannot be contained by even the largest space imaginable as Solomon expresses in 1 Kings 8:27. If God had any size at all, which the Bible does not allude to, then He would have to be bigger than creation which is the universe. That would be an unmeasurable and unfathomable size to our finite human minds! God is everywhere but He acts differently in different places. God can punish in hell, simply sustain the universe like keeping the earth on its axis, or He can bless His creation. God must be present for the universe to exist. He holds everything up with His command (Hebrews 1:3).

GOD IS SPIRIT (John 4:24). God is not flesh and blood. God is spirit. He is not made of any kind of matter. He has no parts or dimensions. Therefore, he cannot be perceived by our human senses. God is greater than all other existence.

GOD IS INVISIBLE (John 1:18). God is invisible. This means that no one has ever seen God in His totality. Even Paul says that God is "unapproachable" and "no one has ever seen Him" (1 Timothy 6:16). God will show Himself to us in limited ways. One way is through created things. For instance, one may find God in nature, human acts of service, or Jesus (who was created in bodily form). There were other appearances of God in the Old Testament. God appeared to Abraham in the form of three men (Genesis 18:1-33), Jacob in the form of a man (Genesis 32:24-30), the people of Israel in a cloud and fire (Exodus 13:21-22), and to Manoah and his wife in the form of an angel (Judges 13:21-22). Moses saw God's face (Exodus 33:20), although God does not have any physical features. Isaiah saw God on a throne wearing a robe (Isaiah 6:1), although God does not wear clothes. There are many more examples. We may never be able to see God entirely but, we can see God truly in whatever form He shows Himself to us. There is no better form than Jesus who is the Christ. When we have known Christ, we have known God.

GOD IS OMNISCIENT (1 John 3:20). Omniscient literally means "all knowing." God knows everything. God knows Himself, which is awesome since He is an eternal and infinite being with no boundaries. God knows everything in the past, present, and future. He also knows all things that are possible. In other words, even if something didn't happen or hasn't happened, He knows what would happen if a particular set of events took place. God knows every star in the sky and every grain of sand on the sea shore. He does not have to recall these facts. He just knows. God knows everything that you are thinking right now and He knows everything that you have ever thought of or will ever think of, not to mention everything that you have done or will do. Therefore, you cannot hide from God. He knows where you are.

GOD IS WISE (Romans 16:27). God's wisdom is different than His knowledge. It means that He always makes wise decisions that brings the best results through the best possible means. The awesome thing is we can ask God for His wisdom in a situation and He will give it to us (James 1:5)! Reading and obeying the word of God is usually how this takes place. God can give you wisdom that is specific to your situation as He did for Solomon during a dispute (1 Kings 3:16-28). Of course, we can never understand all of God's wisdom (Romans 11:33). That is why we often question God as to why He did something or allowed something to happen. God enjoys when His people have faith in His wisdom and have put all of their trust in Him to do the right thing.

GOD IS TRUE (Numbers 23:19). All of God's knowledge, wisdom, and words are true. God is different from mankind in that He has always been and will always be truthful. Indeed, He is the measure of truthfulness and all truths in existence must be compared to Him. God always does what He promises to do.

GOD IS GOOD (Luke 18:19). God is good and is the measure of good in the universe. Everything He does is good. This includes all the things He does or has done that do not seem very good to us at all. Personally, the existence of hell does not seem very good to me but somehow it is, for God can only be good. God is good to those who do not deserve it. Indeed, the fact that you are still breathing right now despite all of the bad things you have done in your life, is proof of God's goodness.

GOD IS LOVE (1 John 4:7-8). God always and forever gives of Himself to people. God is love. For God to stop loving, He would have to stop being God. God embodies love. God invented love. God is love. God does not have to try to love creation. Loving is a part of His being. He cannot help it! God is the measure of love in the universe. Any love that claims to exist must be compared to God, who is the personification of love. Love is an action word to us (1 Corinthians 13) but God is love, literally, not figuratively! This is important to understand. Everything that God says or does is loving. Even that stuff that does not seem loving. Allowing a tsunami to wipe out a community of people does not seem very loving to me but somehow it is! We will never fully understand the love of God but, we may come to know it. God loved you before you ever existed on the planet earth. He already knew who you were and He cherished you before time was (John 17:24). God loved you even when you hated Him, mocked Him, and sinned against Him (Romans 5:8). We can only try and imitate God's love. First we receive God's love for us, then we love Him in return (1 John 4:19), and finally we can love others using God's love (Mark 12:30-31). All the laws of God can be summed up in our love for Him and others. God loves the world (John 3:16), who hates Him, and sent Jesus to save.

GOD IS HOLY (Isaiah 1:4). God is perfect. He will not ever attach Himself to sin. He seeks His own glory and honor at all times. God is holy. That means He is set apart from evil things, actions, people, and thoughts. Mankind is to be holy as well (1 Peter 1:16). That means to be separated from the evil nature of the world and linked to God and His ways. We can only imitate God's holiness. We are not holy in ourselves but we must be holy to commune with God. So, holiness must be bestowed upon us by Jesus upon our repentance and faith in Him (Colossians 1:21-23). Adam and Eve were kicked out of the Garden of Eden after they sinned because God is holy and could no longer directly commune with them. Whenever the Bible describes something as being holy then that means that particular thing or person is set apart for God's own purposes. God is set apart for His own purposes too. God is holy and perfect.

GOD IS RIGHTEOUS (Isaiah 45:19). The root word for "righteous" is "right." Therefore, to be righteous means to be right. How do we know what is right? God is the measure of what is right and, He declares what is right. God is right all the time. So God is righteous. All those who love God are to be righteous too (2 Corinthians 5:21). But how? For mankind to be righteous means for us to be, "rightly aligned," with God or Christ. Righteousness is bestowed upon us through repentance and faith in Christ. Let me explain further. Imagine if someone robs a bank and gets caught. Upon their conviction, they will go to jail because they are no longer righteous or rightly aligned with the government since they broke the law. After they serve their sentence, they are righteous again with the government (in theory) and can go on as if nothing ever happened. No cops would be looking for them nor do they owe anything. They are free. The sentence they served in jail paid for them to regain righteousness. However, speaking of eternity, we need Christ to pay for our righteousness. He did, on the cross. Now you and I have been made right with God and His kingdom and, therefore, have no punishment or condemnation awaiting us for our transgressions. Amen! Considering this example, God is just and will always bring about justice even if it is in ways that we cannot comprehend. Everyone will have their sins paid for either through eternal damnation or faith in Christ. You may not be right but, God has made you right through Christ for His glory. Give Him thanks!

GOD IS JEALOUS (Deuteronomy 4:24). Jealousy is often confused with envy or covetousness. To envy or to covet means to want what another person possesses, either something that is in them or a material thing that they have. To covet my neighbors wife does not mean that I would like to have a wife like her. No! To covet a man's wife means I specifically want his wife. Or maybe I envy the husband who can draw or deserve such a woman. In that case, I probably wish for his destruction. Jealousy, on the other hand, means to be "very watchful" or, "to guard or keep." So if my wife were to kiss another man, I would become very jealous! Why? Because my wife is mine, and I don't want another man to possess her. To covet or envy, is to want something that you don't have or, have rights to. To be jealous is to want to keep something that you do have and is rightfully yours. God is jealous. That means He seeks to protect and keep that which is rightfully his. He wants to protect His elect or chosen people (Ephesians 1:4) who are His possessions and He has a right to. Another possession of God's is His glory or honor. He wants to protect that too. So when people worship idols (Exodus 20:3-5), God gets jealous. He alone deserves worship and praise. When people love His creation more than Him (Romans 1:25), He gets jealous because He alone deserves to be first on the love and honor list. If someone is using God's blessings or anointing, but is not giving God the glory, then he will get jealous since He alone deserves the glory (Isaiah 48:11). And why wouldn't He deserve all these things? He created everything and He loved you when you didn't deserve love. God wants to protect or guard what is His. God is jealous.

GOD IS ANGRY (Exodus 15:7). God intensely hates all sin. Sin is rampant in the world and has been since the very beginning of man. Therefore, God is angry. By the way, God can love and be angry at the same time. The Old Testament speaks often of His anger (Deuteronomy 9:7) but the New Testament does as well (John 3:36). God does not hate people but He does hate sin and the effects of sin. When God's anger falls upon a person it simply means that His righteous judgment has been placed upon a person. God's judgment and anger go together and always results in death. God is angry but, He is very slow to show the effects of His anger (Psalm 103:8-10). He is patient (2 Peter 3:9-10) and gives everyone a chance to repent before His judgment. God will show the effects of His anger during a set and appointed time when He will finally destroy all wickedness. That means eternal damnation for the unsaved. Those who have repented and have faith in Christ need not worry since they have been made right with God through Christ. Whew!

GOD IS PURPOSEFUL (Acts 4:28). God has a purpose in everything that He does. This purpose is usually described as God's will. God's will is all that He wants to do, and is determined to do, in heaven and earth. God's will is all of His activity and existence in the universe. God's will is important. Christ prayed for it to not only reside in heaven but for it to reside on earth (Matthew 6:10). By God's will, He will do everything that He has set out to do (Ephesians 1:11). Sometimes the bad things that happen to God's people are a part of His will for their life (1 Peter 3:17). This is hard to understand but, during these hardships, we must trust God. God has made portions of His will available for us to know and understand but some of His will remains a secret (Deuteronomy 29:29). God willed for Jesus to be killed. Yet He still blamed the people who did it (Acts 2:23). So even though "bad things" may be included in His will, God should never be blamed for evil, sin, or a fallen world. God caused the wickedness of men to work out in His favor when He allowed them to kill Jesus. God does the same thing for us. That is, even the hardships that happen to you will work out for you in the end (Romans 8:28). God's purpose and will is stretched across the universe and no one can stop His advancement. His will is firmly established in heaven. He is currently bringing that establishment down to earth so, all of His people, rejoice!

GOD IS OMNIPOTENT (2 Chronicles 20:6). Omnipotent literally means "all powerful." God is powerful enough to enact and bring to fruition all of His holy will onto earth and in the world. God's power has no limits. Because of His power, nothing is impossible for Him or those who live for Him (Matthew 19:26). God can do anything that He wants to do and no one in heaven or earth could stop Him or challenge Him in anyway. But, He cannot go against His character. He cannot do anything that is not holy, righteous, perfect, just, and so on. He would have to deny Himself in order to do anything like that (2 Timothy 2:13). God will never do that. To deny Himself, He would have to stop being God. In other words, God would have to stop being who He is if He were to go against His character. If you want a full description of God's power (and some other attributes) then read His speech to Job (Job 38). Nothing is too hard for God to accomplish (Jeremiah 32:17). He is the personification of power!

GOD IS HAPPY (Isaiah 62:5). The Bible often says that God is blessed (1 Timothy 1:11). That literally means that God is happy. More specifically, God delights in Himself and in anything else that reflects His character. All the joy that God has is found in Himself. That's why He completely delights in His unique Son, Jesus (Matthew 3:17). God delights in you and me, if His son Jesus abides in us. God's delight and love are two different things. God loved us while we were still sinners (Romans 5:8) but did not delight in us since we were against Him and His ways but, when Jesus resides in us then we become a new creation (2 Corinthians 5:17), spiritually speaking. In other words, when God sees all those who are in Christ, He sees perfection and not our sinful nature. God can be happy and angry at the same time. His passions do not have to be compartmentalized. He is happy with Himself, Jesus, and all who call Jesus, Lord.

GOD IS BEAUTIFUL (Psalm 27:4). God's beauty transcends nature. We see creation as beautiful whether it be a person, a tree, or a horizon. God is not natural and He does not have a body or dimensions of any sort. So God's beauty is not about how He looks, per se. If God's holiness and perfection means that He does not lack anything desirable then His beauty means that He has everything that is desirable. God's beauty is the sum of all that He is. We desire beautiful things. God is all that we should every need to desire. God is beautiful.

GOD IS UNIFIED. God cannot be divided into parts. As humans, who are limited in our ability to understand an eternal God, we must break God up into parts so that we might come to know and understand Him. Much like eating a T-bone steak, one cannot swallow that piece of meat whole. It is necessary to cut it up into pieces before consumption can take place. The reality is that God is all that He is, all at the same time. God is love and light at the same time. Every attribute of God, supports every other attribute since they all make up who God is. Therefore, all of God is angry while all of God is loving. All of God seeks justice, while all of God is patiently waiting for people to repent. It is hard for us to grasp the entirety of God's character all at once. That is why the Bible breaks them up, highlighting each depending on the situation, so that we can focus on portions of God at a time and digest His essence into our spirit. All of His attributes are equally important to God's being. The God of the Old Testament is the exact same unchanging God of the New Testament. Describing His attributes is the only way to tell of who God is and how He is in dealing with His creation. But all of His attributes make up one whole piece that can never be separated or dissected.

One God In Three Persons

As I am writing this book, my target audience are those who have recently decided to follow Jesus the Christ. I do believe this book will be interesting to religious people and all others who are mature in Christ as well. In total, anyone who is in Christ, or think they are in Christ, should find this book very thought provoking. It could even be that one who is unsaved might find this book compelling, since some have chosen not to have faith in Christ due to their lack of interest in the "Church life" style. I think a real depiction of a "Christ centered" lifestyle could pique the interest of those who lack faith. However, it will take the Holy Spirit in your life to help you understand what I am about to explain to you next.

If you are saved through faith in Christ then you also have His spirit, the Holy Spirit, living on the inside of you. Let me explain why you will need God's spirit to understand this portion of the book. It is because it will not make any sense otherwise! You will need the wisdom of God, which comes from the spirit of God, to grasp this foundational biblical teaching. As human beings, we do not know as much as we think we do. That includes scientists, mathematicians, astronomers, geologists, theologians, and any other persons who think they have figured it all out. Mankind only knows what has been discovered. Some of what has been discovered has been misinterpreted. Everything else is a mystery! The sooner you realize just how unlearned you are, the faster you will come into the knowledge of Christ. Indeed, some things man will never find the answers to until God's people meet Him in heaven. Until then, we pray for God to give us revelation. A revelation is when God informs you of something you did not know or was a previously kept secret in heaven. God, give us revelation today!

Grab your Bible or Bible app and follow along with me in 1 Corinthians chapter 2. Starting at verse 4, Paul explains to the audience that he does not speak from his own wisdom, but from God's wisdom which has been given to him (v. 4-6). Paul states that the wisdom of God is a mystery and was previously hidden (v. 7). People who are of the world, a mindset against God, will not understand the mysteries of God (v. 8-9). God revealed these mysteries, or deep secrets, to us by His spirit, the Holy Spirit (v. 10-12). The Holy Spirit is necessary to explain or teach the mysteries of God as well (v. 13). However, the mysteries of God will always sound like foolishness to those who do not have the spirit of God (v. 14-16). In summary, only God can understand God. So you need God on the inside of you so He can explain Himself to you. By His power, your mind can be opened to comprehend such vast and profound secrets. So let's get on with it!

Previously, we have delved into the question, "Who is God?" The answer to that question is too much to consider. So we broke things up into attributes that we may understand. It was not a complete list but a foundational one, none the less. The whole Bible is about God and must be consumed to get the clearest picture possible. Obviously, that is too much for us to deal with in this book. However, there is one more thing about God that I want you to consider at this time. It is the doctrine or teaching of "the Trinity." "Trinity" is not a word that can be found in the Bible. It is a man-made word designed to embody a teaching that permeates across the entire Bible from start to finish. What is the Trinity? It means "tri-unity" or, "three-in-oneness." Wayne Grudem defines it well in the textbook "Bible doctrine: Essential Teachings of the Christian Faith." There he expounds upon the teaching of the Trinity to mean, "God eternally exists as three persons, Father, Son, and Holy Spirit, and each person is fully God, and there is one God."

The important question to consider here is, "How can God be three persons, yet one God?" That is the part that does not make any sense to the rational and natural mind. In other words, The Father is God, Jesus is God, the Holy Spirit is God, and there is only one God. Does that make any sense? This teaching, otherwise called the Godhead, is vital to understanding the divine being of God. One God exists in three persons.

We do not worship or believe in three Gods. We believe in only one God. Remember the attribute of unity? God is not many parts put together. God is one whole being, in three persons. I do not write this to you today out of blind or dumb faith. My faith has been directed by the wisdom of God. You have the wisdom of God available to you too; that is, if you have repented and looked to Jesus for your eternal salvation. So let us lean on the wisdom of God as we endeavor to know the mystery of the Trinity.

God is Three Persons:

Here is fact #1: God is three distinct persons. This fact can be proven in many different places in scripture. Here are a few. John 1:1 says, "In the beginning the Word already existed. The Word was with God, and the Word was God." In verse 14 we can see that the Word became a human. In 1 John 2:1 we read, "…we have an advocate who pleads our case before the Father. He is Jesus Christ…" So, God the Father and Jesus are clearly seen as two persons. Romans 8:27 says, "And the Father who knows all hearts knows what the Spirit is saying, for the Spirit pleads for us believers in harmony with God's own will." In John 14:26 Jesus says, "But when the Father sends the Advocate as my representative—that is, the Holy Spirit—he will teach you everything…" Therefore, the Holy Spirit is clearly not the Father or Jesus. Again, in John 16:7 Jesus promises to send the

Holy Spirit. Many more passages could be listed here that show God is three persons.

I need to emphasize that the Holy Spirit is a person. God is called the Father and Jesus the Son. The Holy Spirit sounds like more of a powerful force or an "it" than a person, but John 14:17 tells us different. Jesus says "**He** is the Holy Spirit, who leads into all truth. The world cannot receive **him**, because it isn't looking for **him** and doesn't recognize **him.** But you know **him**, because **he** lives with you now and later will be in you." This is just one passage that clearly shows the Holy Spirit is indeed a person. The Holy Spirit does everything that the Father and the Son can do such as teaching, praying, speaking, or grieving. The Holy Spirit simply being the power of God is not accurate. The Holy Spirit *has* power (Luke 4:14) just like the Father and the Son.

Each Person is Fully God:

Here is fact #2: The Father is fully God. The Son is fully God. The Holy Spirit is fully God. The Father being God is clearly shown from the very first sentence in the Bible. Jesus prayed to the Father often in scripture. The Father being fully God may be the most obvious fact within this book.

Christ Jesus being fully God can be seen in John 1:1-14. As we read before, the Word was God. The Jehovah's Witnesses translate the original language of this portion of scripture as "The Word was a god." There is a complicated linguistic reason as to why they do this. However, no Greek scholar anywhere agrees or recognizes their reasoning as being true or sound. Also, the same linguistic incident happens other times in scripture but they don't treat those other times the same way and are very inconsistent. It seems John 1:1 did not fit their narrative, so they changed it.

After Jesus was resurrected from the dead, He appeared several times to His disciples. John 20:28 also proves that Jesus is God. On this occasion, Thomas saw Jesus and exclaimed "My Lord and my God!" Hebrews 1:3 mentions that "The Son… expresses the very character of God." The character of God is who He is or embodies His being. If the Son has the character of God then He must be God Himself.

The Holy Spirit being God can be better understood once it is clear that the Father and the Son are each fully God. Matthew 28:19 shows Jesus putting the Holy Spirit on the same level as Him and the Father. It would be absurd for Jesus to do that if the Spirit was merely created. Acts 5:3-4 is another clear example and proof text. Peter accused Ananias of lying to the Holy Spirit in verse 3 and then said that he was lying to God in verse 4. There are passages showing the Holy Spirit as having omnipresence (Psalm 139:7-8) or omniscience (1 Corinthians 2:10-11). God's created things are never all knowing or able to be in multiple places at the same time. Many more passages prove that the Holy Spirit is fully God.

There is One God:

So far things are probably easy to understand. With only the two previous facts to bare, one could safely assume that there are three gods but, that is not true! Here is fact #3: There is only one true God. Now things get really complicated. This fact is repeated three times in Isaiah 45:5-6: "I am the LORD; there is no other God" and again "there is no other God. I am the LORD, and there is no other." Deuteronomy 6:4 says, "The Lord is our God, the LORD alone." Paul claims that "There is only one God" in Romans 3:30. 1 Timothy 2:5 says, "For there is only one God and one Mediator who can reconcile God and humanity—the man Christ Jesus."

How can there be three distinct persons who are fully God and one God? I don't know! But the Bible proves it many more times than I have space to write in this book. Any further proof that one needs has to be provided by the Holy Spirit, God. God can, and will, show Himself to you if you ask Him. First, He'll give you a measure of faith to believe what you have read here and in the Bible. Then, He will help you understand it as far as your natural mind can stand. God is a mystery to us! But facts are facts. God is three persons who are all God but there is only one God.

Alternatives in Error:

There are three teaching errors that offer an alternative to the Trinity doctrine. Each one violates scripture in some way or ignores passages all together. First, Modalism, claims that God is one person who is manifested in three different modes or forms. The thought here is that God is not three distinct persons but actually one person who takes on different forms depending on the place, time, and situation. This belief system is incorrect! Those who adhere to Modalism want to highlight that there is only one God. That is true. So the question is whether God is in distinct modes or persons? Let's investigate!

Go to Matthew 3:13-17 and read the passage. At verse 16, we can see Jesus coming out of the water after His baptism, the Holy Spirit descends from heaven, and a separate voice from heaven (the Father) endorses Jesus by confessing His love and great joy for Him. That is three distinct persons at the same place at the same time! This seems to debunk the theory of God changing from mode to mode when all three personalities are clearly seen having a relationship. There are many other places in the Bible where the Father, Christ, and the Holy Spirit are in the same place at the same time (John 14:16, 2 Corinthians 13:14, Galatians 4:6, Ephesians 2:18, 1 Peter 1:2, Hebrews 9:14, Matthew 28:19). What about the many times that Jesus prayed to God the Father (Matthew 26:39-42, John 17, Mark 6:46, Luke 9:18, Matthew 27:46, Luke 23:46)? Is Jesus praying to

Himself? This would make Jesus seem crazy or schizophrenic with an identity dissociative disorder, right? Tell me, how can Jesus and the Holy Spirit separately pray for us if three distinct personalities are not involved (Romans 8:26, 34). Modalism was invented to try and make sense of something that is counterintuitive. But to exist, it must do harm to what the scriptures plainly show and say. Our brains are designed to make sense of things. However, eternal matters are often outside of our grasp.

The second alternative to the belief in the tri-unity of God is "subordinationism" and can be found in two forms: Adoptionism and Arianism. Both ideas say that Jesus and the Holy Spirit are subordinate to the Father. In regard to Adoptionism, the thought is that Jesus was a great prophet and messiah. The Holy Spirit is reduced to a force or divine power, but not a person. Basically, God raised up Jesus and adopted him as His son. With Arianism, Jesus is more than a human prophet and messiah. However, Jesus is not equal to God. This belief is that Jesus is a secondary god who was created by the Father. Jehovah's Witnesses have taken this belief system even further by saying that Jesus is the incarnation of the archangel Michael. The problem with this is substantial (Philippians 2:6). Only God can save mankind from eternal damnation! If Jesus is not God then we are not saved. Therefore, if Jesus cannot save us then our salvation must come from moralism (trying to be a good person) or legalism (obeying the laws of God). However, mankind is not capable of performing those tasks since perfection is required by God (Romans 8:3, Galatians 2:21). Yes, we are to follow Christ's example, which was perfect, but we cannot measure up to it (Romans 3:23). Jesus saved us because we could not save ourselves. God's thirst for wrath against a sinful people had to be quenched by someone who could pay such a hefty fine. Only God can pay that fine for us, and He did.

The last major alternative to the doctrine of the Trinity is called "tritheism." It states that Father, Son, and Holy Spirit are three separate divine beings. They are not united. They are three different gods altogether. This belief is so far away from the biblical account. In fact, we can see tritheism discussed most often in Christian folk religion or theology. However, tritheism stays alive today, in my opinion, due to poor illustrations that attempt to describe and explain the Trinity. I will discuss some of the better illustrations later but the "egg illustration" of the Trinity is one of the worst. It speaks of the egg as one object that is made up of three parts: a shell, an egg white, and an egg yolk. It is true that all three parts make up one egg. However, the parts are not equal and can be separated. Illustrations like this bring confusion. No illustration works perfectly though. No matter how we try to understand the mystery of the Godhead, the facts about God stated in scripture have to be protected.

Illustrations of Trinity:

Illustrations are a vital mode that humans use to help in under-standing complex ideas about life. That is why I will use illus-trations while describing the gospel. Reading the gospel and seeing it drawn out is very helpful. Breaking the gospel down into an illustration is like simplifying fractions. The fraction 44/68 is hard to understand as it relates to the world. However, 11/17 is much more manageable for our minds to consume. I will list four illustrations here to help us understand the mystery of the Trinity. But I must give you a warning. There is no illustration that can perfectly describe the Trinity for its properties are eternal and infinite which cannot be compared to creation or natural things. All illustrations do some type of disservice to the Godhead but there are some illustrations that are better than others. Just remember that all illustrations fall short of an infinite God and we still need the wisdom of the Holy Spirit in order to understand mysterious ideas.

TRIANGLE. Think about a triangle. It has three equal parts. It is called an equilateral triangle. Each angle is equal at 60 degrees with all three sides equal in length. Now imagine that each of the three vertices or angles represents a member of the Godhead: Father, Son, and Spirit. No matter how you look at the triangle and no matter how you turn the triangle, the figure looks the exact same. This illustration is good at showing three equal parts but only one triangle. However, it falls short since none of the three angles can make a triangle by itself. All three must come together to make a triangle.

THREE RAYS. Since God is light (1 John 1:5), let us look at an illustration that considers light and its three rays. A ray of light is made up of three rays. The first one is called the actinic ray. This ray is invisible to the naked eye. As the ultraviolet part of the spectrum, it is used in radiation. So it has power. But this power cannot be traced by human senses. Only the effects of an actinic ray is noticeable. Second, we consider the aluminiferous ray. When you see light shining on your house, a flash light shining down a dark hallway, or the glow from your smart phone, you are seeing the visible part of the ray called the aluminiferous ray. It is the one that you can see and so it represents the other two rays. Last, we consider the calorific ray. Like the actinic ray, the calorific ray is invisible. However, you can feel its effects. Anytime you feel heat from the sun, a tanning light, or a light bulb, you feeling the heat from the calorific ray. It is the heat ray. You can't see it but you can feel it.

God the Father is like the actinic ray. The Father cannot be seen (1 Timothy 1:17) but He is still God who has power. The Father is constantly working but His work goes unnoticed by humans. For instance, the fact that life still exists in the universe is the constant work of the Father.

The Son, Jesus, is like the aluminiferous ray. Jesus is the member of the Godhead that can be seen by the naked eye (Colossians 1:15). Let me clarify. Jesus is in heaven now so we cannot see Him but when He was on the planet people could, and when He returns, He will look just as He did during His ministry on earth. Jesus is fully a man (while also being fully God). So, we can see, notice, and recognize Him. Since we relate better to Jesus, He represents God to us. He talks, walks, and breathes like we do. Our senses can consume Him in that way.

The Holy Spirit is like the calorific ray. It is invisible as well but we can feel it (Acts 1:8). Like the wind that is invisible, we can feel its effects. Heat cannot be seen but it can be felt.

Light has an invisible ray, a visible ray, and an invisible heat ray. But they are collectively called light. Each one is light by itself. Each one is equal to the others. The only differences are how each relate to creation. Light has three distinct and inseparable parts that we collectively call "Light."

THREE DIMENSIONS OF MAN. All human beings have two parts: body and soul/spirit. The body is a machine. The spirit is the life force of man which contains a soul. The soul carries the wants and desires of man which could otherwise be known as "consciousness" or "self-awareness." The soul/spirit is who we are apart from the body. Let me explain. When you die, your body lies in a casket. Your soul/spirit is absent (2 Corinthians 5:8). When people look at your dead body, they call you by name. Your soul/spirit, however, gives the body life. It is who you are. When people are in a coma and on life support, the body is alive but the soul is inactive. So that person has no real life until they come out of the coma. If you are saved and your body dies, your soul/spirit separates from the body and goes to heaven. But this is only because the (Holy) Spirit has been added to the group. Therefore, upon salvation, you are no longer body and soul/spirit. You are body, soul/spirit, and Holy Spirit. [Note: The Bible calls your "consciousness" while connected to the body, "soul." When referring to you apart from the body, the Bible calls it "spirit" with a lower case "s." Therefore, "Spirit" with an uppercase "S" always refers to the Holy Spirit in particular. However, the soul and spirit are not exactly the same thing. But they are so closely related and similar that I combined them here.]

It is important to notice that when you are alive, your body, soul/spirit, and Holy Spirit are seen as one being. You. Your body, your soul/spirit, and the Spirit of God are all seen as one person. Only death can separate them for they are one person. Each one is distinct from one another yet your friends look at you and see only one person. No one says hello to your body, then says hello to your soul/spirit, and then says hello to the Spirit of God in you. They just say hello to you.

The main reason that this illustration falls short is because, unlike the Godhead of the Trinity, our body, soul/spirit, and Spirit (of God) are not in perfect unity. The Father, Son, and Holy Spirit are in perfect tri-unity. We are not like that, unfortunately. Our body gets information from a sinful world (Romans 8:13). The soul is gullible and likes the sinful information, most of the time (Romans 3:23). The Holy Spirit understands the desire for sin as false information. The Spirit tells the soul that the information is incorrect. The soul is then commissioned to tell the body to stop translating the sinful desires into actions. This is a conflict and fight that every disciple of Christ will have with themselves until they die and become totally perfected in heaven.

WATER. All living things need water (John 4:7-14). Water does not have any form. One cannot hold it using an open palm. However, one can hold an ice cube. Ice does have form no matter where you see it. Steam does not have form either but it does bring heat. This heat (power) can be used to move a locomotive. Steam is invisible. What we can see is actually water vapor, little water droplets that are in the air. Steam, on the other hand, is water heated to the point that is turns into invisible gas. Formless H_2O is water. Frozen H_2O is water. Evaporated H_2O is water. We can't hold God the Father in our hand. But we can hold Jesus for He is man. The Holy Spirit cannot be held but He gives us power (Acts 1:8). Formless water, ice, and steam are the same chemical substance, water.

The Importance of the Doctrine of the Trinity:

Why is it important to believe in the Trinity? Can we not just believe in God however we want to? Maybe we can just believe in Jesus and call it even, right? What difference does it make as long as you believe in God? If we cannot fully understand God anyway then why can't we just pick a way to view God and stick with it? If all three persons are God then can't we just pick one to focus on? These are all really good questions.

The main reason the atonement is so vital is because the atonement is the reconciliation of God and humankind through Jesus Christ. It takes all three persons of the Godhead to be fully God but one God for us to be saved. They all play a vital role but only God can save us.

This is how the process of atonement works. All of mankind needs to get back into communion with God in order to have life, purpose, and significance. The problem is that no one can come to God on their own. They must use a Mediator. If God the Father takes us directly then He would have to enact justice upon us, which is death, the penalty for sin (Romans 6:23). Jesus is the Mediator between God and man (1 Timothy 2:5). So Jesus explained things to us by saying, "I am the Way, the truth, and the life. No one can come to the Father except through me." (John 14:6). There is a caveat to that, though. Jesus explained further in John 6:44: "For no one can come to me unless the Father who sent me draws them to me, and at the last day I will raise them up."

We all need to get back to God but can only do it through one man, Jesus. The Father sent the Son and now we can see the Son sending the Holy Spirit. In John 16:7 Jesus said, "But in fact, it is best for you that I go away, because if I don't, the Advocate won't come. If I do go away, then I will send him to you." In verse 8, we can see one reason why the Holy Spirit must be sent: "And when he comes, he will convict the world of its sin, and of God's righteousness, and of the coming judgment." The original Greek word (elegcho) that is translated into "convict" can also mean "to convince." So, mankind must be convicted (shown to be wrong and feel shame), and convinced that they need a Savior. The Holy Spirit does that work through men and women of God as Paul stated in 2 Corinthians 5:18-20. After conviction, one can confess and believe that Jesus is Lord and that God raised Him from the dead (Romans 10:9). Then we can be saved.

One can begin to see how the process of atonement is interwoven amongst the three persons of the Godhead. We need the Father but He can't keep us or He'll have to kill us. He knows you need Jesus to atone for sin but at that point, Jesus is not ready to take you because you must be convicted first. So the Holy Spirit takes you, but He cannot keep you. He must send you to the Son. Jesus, the Mediator, then sends you to the Father. We are back in communion with the Father but that's still not enough. We need Jesus to teach and be an example for us on how to overcome the world. The Holy Spirit gives us power so we can live a godly life and please God (2 Peter 1:3). The atonement is something that only God can lead us through. All three persons of the Trinity are fully God: the Father, Son, and Spirit.

THE PERSON OF CHRIST

I almost did not write this chapter. What a great mistake that would have been! Why should Christ get a chapter all to Himself? It is not because He is more important than the Father or the Holy Spirit. We just finished discussing how they are equal in stature. The Father, Son, and Spirit are one. They are distinctly different and one in the same. However, from a limited human perspective, there is one that stands out.

The biggest reason why Christ is the focal point of all who believe in the God of the Bible is because He is a human being! That means He looks like us, talks like us, and walks like us. Therefore, we can relate to Him and attempt to get to know Him easier. For instance, we can better understand that Jesus is our friend because humans are often friends of each other. Jesus relates to humans as any other human does. The Father is our friend and the Holy Spirit is our friend too but we cannot see them or relate to them since they are not human. We have the chance to read in the Bible and see how Jesus relates to people in a face to face manner. Jesus cried when Lazarus died (John 11:32-35). Jesus experienced turmoil like we do (Luke 22:44). Jesus became hungry (Mathew 4:2), tired (John 4:5-6), and thirsty (John 19:28). Starting from the form of a baby, Jesus had to learn and gather information just as we do (Luke 2:52). Maybe the greatest attribute that Jesus shares with us as a human being is that He could die or be killed (John 19:30-33). So it is clear why many tend to focus on Jesus more often than the Father or the Holy Spirit.

There is a big question that needs to be addressed. How can Jesus be a human and God at the same time? Is Jesus 50% man and 50% God, or is it some other division of 100% (Apollinarianism)? Was Jesus God (the Word), at first (John 1:1-5), and then became only human (verse 14)? Are there two separate persons in Jesus that do not combine, which allows Him to function in one or the other at any given time (Nestorianism)? Could it be that the divine nature that Jesus had before time, combined with the human nature He received upon His birth, made an entirely new nature altogether (Monophysitism)?

In 451 A.D. there was a response given to answer such divisive questions concerning Christ's nature. An orthodox view point and response was agreed upon and penned during the Fourth Ecumenical Council which was held in Chalcedon (currently Turkey). "Ecumenical" simply means a combination of all or a vast majority of Christian churches and denominations. "Orthodox" just means generally accepted as right or true. The statement is not long. I will list it here in its totality; although, it is paraphrased from old English for greater clarity. The original Creed of Chalcedon can be googled very easily. Then we can discuss the person of Christ in further detail. The creed reads as follows:

THE CREED

Therefore, following the holy fathers, we all with one accord teach men to acknowledge one and the same Son, our Lord Jesus Christ, at once complete in Godhead and complete in manhood, truly God and truly man, consisting also of a reasonable soul and body; of one substance with the Father as regards his Godhead, and at the same time of one substance with us as regards his manhood; like us in all respects, apart from sin; as regards his Godhead, begotten of the Father before the ages, but yet as regards his manhood begotten, for us men and for our salvation, of Mary the Virgin, the God-bearer; one and the same Christ, Son, Lord, Only-begotten, recognized in two natures, without confusion, without change, without division, without separation; the distinction of nature's being in no way annulled by the union, but rather the characteristics of each nature being preserved and coming together to form one person and subsistence, not as parted or separated into two persons, but one and the same Son and Only-begotten God the Word, Lord Jesus Christ; even as the prophets from earliest times spoke of him, and our Lord Jesus

Christ himself taught us, and the creed of the fathers has handed down to us.

Christ as Human:

We know that Jesus is a human because He was born of a woman. This account can be read at the beginning of the book of Matthew and Luke. The only difference between Jesus' birth and ours is that His mother, Mary, was not given a human seed. The seed that she was impregnated with was literally from God the Father by the work of the Holy Spirit (Matthew 1:18). Jesus had an earthly father, Joseph, who did not provide a seed for Mary to incubate. In order to prove that Mary did not receive a seed from a man, God chose a virgin. In Jewish culture, the lady had to be a virgin before she married. That is why, when she became pregnant, Joseph wanted to call off the wedding because he obviously thought she had slept with a man (Matthew 1:18-25). Once Joseph found out otherwise, he did not sleep with Mary until after Jesus was born. Again this would prove that her seed could not have come from a man. However, like all mothers, Mary held Jesus in her womb for a full term and had a natural birth. As a baby, Jesus was a helpless human being in that He needed His mother to feed, clothe, hold, soothe, and clean Him.

The virgin birth is necessary because that is when God the Word, became a man. There are other things to consider here. First, we can see that salvation can only come from the Lord. Mary could not conceive Jesus, the Savior of the world, on her own effort. The Holy Spirit did the work. Secondly, the virgin birth made it possible to unite full deity and full humanity into one person. Basically Jesus, who was the Word, was given human DNA from Mary. Yet He maintained His original "DNA," so to speak, which provided the opportunity to be fully man and fully God at the same time. This is not how nature usually works. For instance, when an African-American person mates with a Caucasian person then a brand new ethnicity is created as the two originals combine. In Jesus' case, His two natures miraculously maintained their distinctiveness. Thirdly, the virgin birth makes it possible for Jesus to inherit humanity from Mary but not her sinfulness, which all humans inherit from the first man, Adam (Romans 5:12-19). Plus, we know that God can have no sin in Him (Habakkuk 1:13).

The Bible clearly confirms that Jesus was sinless while He lived upon the earth. Jesus was sent into the wilderness to be tempted by Satan (Luke 4:1-13) to sin against His Father in heaven. Satan was not successful in his attempt. Later, Jesus asked His opponents if they could accuse Him of any sin (John 8:46). He received no answer. Pontius Pilate found no fault in Him and admittedly crucified an innocent man (John 18:38; Matthew 27:24). The Bible says that Jesus never sinned (2

Corinthians 5:21, 1 Peter 2:22, 1 John 3:5) and was perfect (1 Peter 1:19). Furthermore, Jesus faced all of the same temptations that we face; however, He did not sin (Hebrews 4:15)! Because of these experiences, Jesus can understand our weaknesses and help us during temptation (Hebrews 2:18).

Jesus' temptations were not exactly like ours but they were very similar. Let's consider what He was tempted with by Satan (Luke 4). Jesus was tempted to eat when His Father very clearly told Him not to. Remember, Jesus' body was just like ours. It needed to eat. Jesus felt pain and weakness. Trust me! Jesus wanted to eat right then but He wanted to do the will of His Father even more. That is why Jesus said, "People do not live by bread alone" (verse 4). In other words, the body needs food but it is better to please the giver of life who can create life out of nothing, raise up a dead body, and cause someone to live forever. In the same way, humans need water to live but God can provide for man in such a way that natural water is not needed (John 4:7-14).

Next, Jesus was tempted to bypass His earthly ministry, torture, and death with an offer to receive all the kingdoms of the world by worshipping Satan (verse 6-7). Jesus' purpose was to eventually rule all of the nations (as He does today from heaven and will one day in person). That is what made this such a great temptation. Jesus knew that it was better to suffer and please God then to gain the world through evil means. Lastly, Satan tempted Jesus to reveal His full deity (as He did on the mountain during the Transfiguration in Matthew 17:1-8). Satan baited Jesus to jump from a high point and let His angels save Him but Jesus knew it was not time to fully reveal Himself to the world (as He may have preferred). For example, before Jesus was arrested by Roman soldiers, one of His disciples cut off the ear of the high priest's slave but Jesus rebuked the disciple by saying, "Don't you realize that I could ask my Father for thousands of angels to protect us, and he would send them instantly?" (Matthew 26:51-53). Overall, Jesus was tempted to do things other than what God wanted Him to do. This is the foundation of all sin. However, Jesus never did sin!

Jesus being a human is very necessary and vital in the work of salvation. First, mankind needed a new representative. Our first one was Adam. Read Romans 5:12-21 for better clarity. Verse 15 says, "But there is a great difference between Adam's sin and God's gracious gift. For the sin of this one man, Adam, brought death too many. But even greater is God's wonderful grace and his gift of forgiveness to many through this other man, Jesus Christ." Sin entered the world when Adam and Eve were tested in the Garden. Yet Jesus passed His test in the wilderness. Through Adam's disobedience, we are sinful creatures, but through Jesus' obedience, we are made righteous or friends of God.

Secondly, we needed a sinless sacrifice as a substitute for our sinful lives and ways. However, the only one who can be considered perfect is God. God cannot die so He had to become a man that could die for our sins. Isn't that awesome! Thirdly, Jesus needed to be a human so that He could represent us before God. The Bible calls Him our mediator (1 Timothy 2:5) or High Priest (Hebrews 4:14-16). In the Old Testament, a priest could commune with God. We have all been made priests through Jesus (1 Peter 2:9). In the Old Testament, a high priest would represent all of the people to God (Leviticus 4:3-21, Exodus 30:10, Leviticus 16:14-15). Now our High Priest is Jesus. Read the whole chapter of Hebrews 9 for greater clarity. Basically, mankind is sinful and cannot commune with God but just as a lawyer speaks for his client in court, Jesus represents us before God. Therefore, His purity is on display instead of our sin. This makes us righteous before God. Amen!

Christ as Deity (God):

During our discussion of the Godhead or Trinity, we covered the fact that Jesus is God along with the Father and the Holy Spirit but it is important to reiterate the case for Christ as God here again. There are several scriptures that explicitly state that Jesus is God. These New Testament scriptures use a Greek word, *Theos,* that is translated into our English equivalent, God. *Theos* is usually used to describe the Father but is also used to describe Jesus. New Testament examples of the use of *Theos* are: John 1:1, 1:18, 20:28; Romans 9:5; Titus 2:13; Hebrews 1:8; and 2 Peter 1:1. We can also examine an Old Testament passage, Isaiah 9:6, which describes Jesus as a "Mighty God."

Christ is often described as being the Lord. The Septuagint, which is the Greek translation of the Old Testament, translates the Greek word *kyrios* as Lord. Let it be noted that this translation was commonly used during Christ's life on earth. The Septuagint uses *kyrios* whenever God, commonly known as Father, Creator, Yahweh, or Jehovah, is the subject.

Before we go any further, let me first explain what a "lord" is. To be specific, I am referring to a lord within a kingdom, which is the type of government that God governs. In a kingdom there is only one lord, the king. That is because the king is the only one who owns anything. A king owns everything within his territory. That includes all of the land, everything on the land, and the people. The citizens do not own anything! There is no such thing as personal property. They are merely stewards of what the lord or king allows them to use. Furthermore, the lord, or king, can redistribute his property to whomever he wants whenever he wants. All of these facts describe a king's lordship. In other words, a king owns everything in his domain or kingdom. So far I have been using a lower case "l" in the word lord. However, God is the Lord, capital "L." He is the ultimate Lord. In other words, God is Lord of all the lords (1 Timothy 6:15)! Therefore, lords are simply stewards of the Lords property which, in God's case, is everything in the universe including the whole earth (1 Corinthians 10:26). To be clear, your confession of faith that Jesus is Lord, is to say that He owns you and everything that you have.

You may have possession of a deed or a title, but you should stop viewing yourself as a REAL owner! Owners have to fight for everything that they get and are frightened that they might lose it all due to economic crisis, inflation, or theft. In God's kingdom there can never be an economic crisis or shortage of any kind. Upon our confession of faith, we are relieved of any stress about how we are going to live or make it in life since we don't depend on ourselves or our resources. We depend on God and His resources which do not diminish. God's people may not own anything but, they have access to everything! Would you rather own that plot of land that you have or, give that up in order to have access to any of God's infinite resources that He makes available to you?

Considering all of this, let's return to our discussion of Jesus as Lord. My absolute favorite scripture proving this point can be found in Luke 19:30-31. Jesus spoke to two of His disciples and commanded them to "Go into that village over there" and "As you enter it, you will see a young donkey tied there that no one has ever ridden. Untie it and bring it here. If anyone asks, 'Why are you untying that colt?' just say, 'The Lord needs it.'" Notice that Jesus did not tell the men to ask for the colt but to demand it by using the authority of the Lord as owner. There would be no need to argue since the Lord owns everything.

There are other New Testament examples. Luke 2:11 refers to Jesus as Lord when He was a baby. That is significant! Jesus did not have to earn such status since He always had it since before time. Mathew 3:3 refers to a prophecy that Isaiah spoke in the Old Testament about John the Baptist calling Jesus Lord even before His ministry began officially. Matthew 22:44 shows Jesus reasoning with some religious leaders by quoting something that David said in the Old Testament about the coming Messiah being Lord. In 1 Corinthians 8:6 and 12:3, Jesus is closely compared to the Father and Holy Spirit, respectively, and given the title of Lord in both instances.

The claims of Jesus are very important. We all need to consider that He is either Lord, liar, or lunatic. By faith, one must choose which he or she will believe. And yes, it does require faith to believe Jesus is a liar or a lunatic when you consider the mounting evidence to the contrary. Jesus' claims of Himself were considered blasphemy during His day. It is ultimately what got Him killed.

There were many times when Jesus claimed to be God. Let's consider just three of them here. First, in John chapter 8, Jesus makes certain claims right in front of the religious leaders of the day. But none were more shocking than the last one that He made. Jesus mentioned that Abraham, who had died centuries before, had rejoiced when thinking of Jesus and His coming to the earth (verse 56). The religious leaders knew this could not be possible since Abraham and Jesus lived hundreds of years apart. Jesus responded in verse 58, "I tell you the truth, before Abraham was even born, I AM!" Everyone knew that Jesus was claiming to be God. The Father had identified

Himself to Abraham (Exodus 3:14) as "I AM WHO I AM." Furthermore, Jesus could have said "Before Abraham was even born, I was" but instead said "I AM." This shows an explicit attempt in claiming to be God.

Secondly, Jesus made a claim by saying, "I am the Alpha, and the Omega, the First and the Last, the Beginning and the End" (Revelation 22:13). Jesus made the similar statement in Revelation 1:8 while claiming to be The Mighty One. So, clearly, Jesus refers to Himself in the same context as the Father does.

Third, Jesus claims to be the Son of God. It is important to understand that every human being on the planet is a son of God since He created everyone. Also, consider that a redeemed person, or one who has found salvation in Jesus, is specifically called sons of God in certain translations. Even the nation of Israel is called a son of God in Hosea 11:1. But, "Son of God," can also, specifically, refer to Jesus. Let's look at a famous verse of scripture in John 3:16. Here, Jesus is call God's "only begotten Son," or "one and only Son." While taking other scriptures into consideration, one can see that this is not true. The fact is that most Bibles translate this verse incorrectly. The original word used is *monogenes* which means "single of its kind." The word "kind" refers to the human race and "single" refers to Jesus. In other words, Jesus is God's "Unique Son." That means there is no other son that God has who is like or even comparable to Jesus. Therefore, we can see Jesus making this claim in Matthew 11:27. The Father made the same claim in

Matthew 17:5 after Jesus' baptism. The same claim is made by the apostles (1 Corinthians 15:28, Hebrews 1:1-3, 5, 8). I don't think any place in scripture explains this any better than John chapter 1. There Jesus is seen as the Word and Son who existed along with God the Father in eternity.

The deity of Jesus is very necessary. First, only someone who is the infinite God could bear the sins of the entire world. Second, only God can bring salvation to mankind. Third, only someone who is God could approach the Father and be a Mediator between God and man.

The God Man:

Considering what has been discussed above, one should consider Jesus to be fully God and fully man. That is to say Jesus is 100% God, and 100% human. How can this be? I don't know! The human mind and its limitations will never be able to understand totally until we see God face to face. Jesus is not like Dr. Jekyll and Mr. Hyde. Those two persons had to take turns assuming control and authority. Jesus is 100% human all the time and 100% God all the time! This is truly a mystery.

How does the atonement work?

The work that Jesus did during His life and death on earth to earn our salvation caused Him to become "the atonement." The word atonement in the Bible has been translated from the Hebrew word, *kaphar*, meaning, "To cover." Here is a quick history lesson. First, God covered the sin and shame of Adam and Eve when He placed an animal skin over them. Let it be noted that an innocent animal had to die for this to take place. That represented the very first blood shed of any kind in creation. Adam and Even both deserved to be immediately put to death for their treason but God killed an animal instead and used that death to, literally, cover their sins. Now their nakedness could not be seen even though it was still there. This continued throughout the Old Testament (Leviticus 1:4-5, 17:11) and until Jesus' resurrection. Basically, an innocent animal always had to die to atone, or cover, the wrong doings of the people. These sacrifices, or killings, had to happen over and over and over again because the people continually sinned. However, ultimately, these sacrifices could not properly atone for sins from an eternal perspective (Hebrews 10:4). Man needed a better sacrifice.

Mankind needed a Messiah or Christ! First, let's discuss how people call Him, "Jesus Christ." This is just fine as long as it is understood that "Christ," is not Jesus' last name. Christ refers to His title or authority. Therefore, it is more appropriate to call Him Jesus the Christ. No one would call Him "Jesus Messiah." They would say Jesus the Messiah. The word "Christ" comes from *christos*, a Greek word meaning "anointed." It is the equivalent of the Hebrew word, *mashiach*, which is translated "Messiah." Therefore, to call Jesus the Christ is to say that He is the anointed One of God.

What does "anointed" mean? To be anointed is to have sacred oil poured on one's head. This would happen if someone was chosen for a special task. Priests or prophets could be anointed but to say, "anointed one," would usually refer to a king. They had oil poured on their head during coronation instead of receiving a crown. So the imagery of the word, "Christ," is to paint the picture of an anointed king that has been chosen by God. Jesus the Christ (Messiah) was prophesied about many times in the Old Testament (i.e. Micah 5:2, Deuteronomy 18:18, Isaiah 7:14, 11:1-4). Maybe the most noticeable prophesy is in Isaiah 52:13 - 53:12 where Christ's atonement for our sins is front and center while speaking of His suffering to come. Today we can still anoint with oil, but now it has more of a spiritual connection then a natural one. In other words, to be anointed of God is to be chosen for a special task where God has poured Himself onto you or empowered you for the job. Just because someone can sing well or preach well does not necessarily mean they are anointed. They may just be displaying great talent. However, a true anointing will always point people towards Jesus by using the gifts of the Spirit.

Now let's continue with our discussion of the atonement. Mankind needed a better sacrifice that could cover sin once and for all. We needed Jesus the Christ, who the prophets spoke of concerning His coming and suffering for our sins. But did He have to die? Yes! Let me explain. Mankind sinned against God. Therefore, man had to suffer the consequences

of sin, which is death. God is just. That means He has to punish wrong doings. Much like someone on death row today, the
sinner dying makes him right again with the government but,
now that he is dead, he cannot reap the benefits of a payed
off penalty! Furthermore, God wants man to live so, man cannot pay this penalty of death. Therefore, God created a system
where a sinner must die for his or her actions or, another can
die in their place. In other words, another can represent the
sinner in death, so the actual sinner will not have to die since
something died for them. But animal sacrifices were not good
enough for eternal purposes. The animals were not a worthy
sacrifice. God wanted sin to be dealt with for past, present, and
future actions.

Only God could pay the penalty for sin but this was a
problem. First, God is perfect and therefore did not owe such a
price or penalty. Second, God does not have the ability to die!
Mankind deserved the penalty for sin but could not pay it. God
wanted to pay for the sin but He had not done anything wrong
nor did He have the ability to die for the sins. So God planned
the whole thing! He decided that He would wrap Himself in
flesh and come to earth in the likeness of man. In this way He
could take on the humanity, hardship, temptations, death, and
other frailties of mankind. This includes sin!

How can a perfect God take on sin? This is where the
fullness of Christ's humanity and deity come into play. First,
Jesus could take on sin through His natural, inherited, body.

We know that He never sinned, but Jesus had a body corrupted with sin and gave Him the ability to die, which is the penalty for sin. Second, since Jesus never sinned, He was a perfect and spotless sacrifice who, as a human, could totally represent mankind and, as a sinless person, could be worthy to be an adequate sacrifice that would appease the Father's anger towards sin and save all who believe in the Christ. Remember, God had always used spotless or innocent animals during sacrifices. Now Jesus could be that innocent Lamb (John 1:29).

You are a sinner! You should have died on that cross! That is what you earned for yourself and deserve based on the life you and your fore father, Adam, have lived. But instead, Jesus died there, in your place. In other words, Jesus, representing you and all the wrong you have ever done or will do, died on the cross. In doing so, Jesus covered for your sin. When a friend does not tell on you or turn you into the authorities after a transgression, he has covered for you. That is what Jesus did for all of us, except, He did it legally. Jesus perfectly administered the God given mercy of sacrifices, and He did it for you when you did not even love Him! He showed His love for you first (Romans 5:8, 1 John 4:19) by dying when He did nothing wrong to deserve or earn such a penalty. Now you are considered a friend of God (upon your repentance and confession of Jesus as Lord) and have been made righteous in God's eyes. In other words, God now will treat you, who are a sinner, like you are perfect and have never sinned. This is because Jesus the

Christ is your representative in heaven. That means He stands before God representing you in His perfection! You are eternally blessed! You did not do this, Christ did this for you. This is because He loves you! That is how the atonement works.

His Resurrection:

Christ's work on the earth and His atonement for our sins was not complete until He came back to life again. The New Testament speaks about His resurrection repeatedly (Matt. 28:1-20, Mark 16:1-8, Luke 24:1-53, John 20:1-21:25). It is important to notice that Jesus' resurrection was not simply Him just coming back from the dead like Lazarus did (John 11:1-44). That is because Lazarus still eventually died, as all people do. Jesus was to be the first of a new type of resurrection that, not only gave new life, but a new perfected body incapable of dying. Read 1 Corinthians chapter 15 for great clarity about the resurrection of Jesus, those to come later, and the new spiritual bodies that will be inherited.

Jesus was raised back to life. It is important to realize that Jesus was raised all while maintaining His humanity. In other words, Jesus was raised back to life with a human body that looked the same as it did when He was put to death. When Jesus first appeared after His resurrection, some did not recognize Him at first (Luke 24:13-32, John 20:14-16). Still, they soon saw Him as they knew Him to be. Many other times, whoever saw Him would recognize His face pretty quickly (Matt. 28:9, 17; John 20:19-20, 26-28; 21:7, 12).

There are several pieces of evidence that show Jesus as a human with a body after His resurrection. I will list a few here: the disciples took hold of His feet (Matt. 28:9), Jesus ate food (Luke 24:30, 42-43; John 21:12-13, Acts 10:41), and Jesus' perfected body still showed the wounds that He was given during His crucifixion (John 20:20, 27). However, Luke 24:39 shows Jesus plainly stating this fact when He told the disciples: "Look at my hands. Look at my feet. You can see that it's really me. Touch me and make sure that I am not a ghost, because ghosts don't have bodies, as you see that I do."

Jesus was still a human after His resurrection even though He was able to appear and reappear very quickly. At times it seemed like Jesus disappeared, but these are just miraculous happenings which have happened before. Consider that Elijah was taken away to heaven in a chariot (2 Kings 2:11) and Philip disappeared after baptizing a eunuch (Acts 8:39).

It is best to conclude that the Father and the Son took part in the resurrection. And if they took part in the resurrection then so must have the Holy Spirit. There are texts that confirm the Father raising Jesus from the dead (Acts 2:24, Romans 6:4, 1 Corinthians 6:14). However, Jesus clearly states in John 10:17-18 "The Father loves me because I sacrifice my life so I may take it back again. No one can take my life from me. I sacrifice it voluntarily. For I have the authority to lay it down when I want to and also to take it up again. For this is what my Father has commanded." Jesus also alluded to this in John 2:19-21 when He spoke of the destruction of the temple.

There are several reasons why the resurrection of Christ Jesus is necessary for our renewed lives as believers. First, God sees all those who believe in Christ as being raised up with Him during His resurrection. Ephesians 2:6 says, "For he raised us from the dead along with Christ and seated us with him in the heavenly realms because we are united with Christ Jesus." Therefore, we have been given power! Paul states that his goal in life is, "I want to know Christ and experience the mighty power that raised him from the dead." (Philippians 3:10). Paul also said, "I also pray that you will understand the incredible greatness of God's power for us who believe him. This is the same mighty power that raised Christ from the dead and seated him in the place of honor at God's right hand in the heavenly realms" (Ephesians 1:19-20). This power is available to people so that they can now accomplish that which they could not previously accomplish. There is no better example than our victory over sin and death. Christ's resurrection gives us power to overcome sin and death (Romans 6:4, 11, 17; 1 Corinthians 15:17). This power has also been given to us for ministry (Acts 1:8). God's resurrection power in our lives allows us the ability to perform miracles, healings, give words of wisdom and knowledge, and activate other fruits of the spirit (Galatians 5:22-23) which can ultimately lead someone to Christ. So, make a list of everything that you cannot do for Christ. Now God's resurrection power can be released in your life. That way you can perform for God on earth just as Jesus did. And all things will be possible with God (Matthew 19:26, Mark 9:23).

Secondly, Christ's resurrection means that we are justified. To justify means to prove to be right or righteous. To be righteous is to be in good standing with the government of God. For instance, if you are caught speeding then you will receive a ticket to appear in court. You are no longer righteous or right aligned with the government. After you pay the fine, or court costs, you are made righteous again or seen as innocent by the government. This is by your own efforts. But for eternal things, we cannot pay our own fine. Christ did this for us. Wayne Grudem says it best in his book, Bible Doctrine: Essential Teachings of the Christian Faith: "By raising Christ from the dead, God the Father was in effect saying that he approved of Christ's work of suffering and dying for our sins, that his work was completed, and that Christ no longer had any need to remain dead. There was no penalty left to pay for sin, no more wrath of God to bear, no more guilt or liability to punishment—all had been completely paid for and no guilt remained." Since we have all been raised with Christ, then we are justified or have been made right with God. Just as Christ has no further work to do, neither do we because He has done all of the work for us! It is finished! That is why Paul said, "He was raised to life to make us right with God" in Romans 4:25.

Third, since Jesus received a perfected new body, so will we. Jesus' body had scars left on it. He particularly had some on His feet, hands, and side. However, we must remember that the beating He received was brutal. He had damage all over His body and the flesh was literally dangling off of Him, but all of that damage was healed. For Christ, those other scars were left so that His disciples would recognize Him and see that His body had been resurrected. For us, our bodies will be free of any damage, decay, or disease gathered in our lifetime (1 Corinthians 15).

Fourth, Christ's resurrection gives us hope. We have hope that no matter what happens to us in this life, we are assured an eternal life with new bodies. After speaking of the resurrection, Paul says in 1 Corinthians 15:58, "So, my dear brothers and sisters, be strong and immovable. Always work enthusiastically for the Lord, for you know that nothing you do for the Lord is ever useless." That is because, no matter what happens in this life, it will inevitably lead to a resurrection for the believer. Therefore live without fear and be steadfast in your work for Christ. Also, we should think about our eternal future when the trials and hardships of life try to knock us down.

After Christ's resurrection, He ascended to heaven (Luke 24:51, Acts 1:9-11). He received glory and honor in such a way that He had never had before as a God-man (John 17:5, Philippians 2:9, 1 Timothy 3:16). All of this culminated when He received the seat at the right hand of the Father (Ephesians

1:20-21, 1 Peter 3:22, Acts 2:33). At that point, Jesus could announce to His disciples in Matthew 28:18, "I have been given all authority in heaven and on earth."

Christ Jesus' ascension into heaven with glory, honor and authority is very important to our life here on earth. First, since we are united with Christ, we are assured that we too will see heaven, just as He has (1 Thessalonians 4:17, 2 Corinthians 5:8). There is no better affirmation of our place in heaven than when Jesus said in John 14:2-3, "There is more than enough room in my Father's home. If this were not so, would I have told you that I am going to prepare a place for you? When everything is ready, I will come and get you, so that you will always be with me where I am." Wow! Trust in Jesus' words, my friends.

Secondly, we share in His authority. Remember, we are heirs with Christ (Romans 8:17). Christ is the lead heir or the first born Son (of many to come) but we share in His inheritance. That includes, among other things such as suffering, His authority. Those who endure with Christ are promised "authority over all the nations," and to "rule the nations," because we will have the "same authority [Jesus] received" (Revelations 2:26-28). Furthermore, we will sit with Christ on His throne (Revelation 3:21). Some of these things refer to our eternal future. However, we have authority now that has been given to us by Christ. When we say, "in Jesus name," we are using His authority to cast out a demon, bring about healing, or speak with the Father. The phrase, "in Jesus name," is not a magic trick but, as His children, gives us the use of Christ's authority. When a child tells a sibling "Dad told me to tell you to come here," the child has no authority to command the sibling, but the dad does. So the child used the dad's name to command the sibling. The dad gave the child permission to use his name in that situation. Christ has done the same for us! We don't really have authority but Christ does. He has given us permission to use His name or authority (John 14:13-14) in certain situations.

SALVATION ILLUSTRATIONS

I love to watch super hero movies with my wife and three children. There are millions all over the world who can relate to this feeling. The Marvel studios alone have grossed over 7 billion dollars of revenue in its recent history. DC comics is not far behind with over 5 billion dollars in gross revenue. However, these two companies only represent a portion of the super hero movies that hit the box office year after year. Not all super hero movies involve people with "super powers." Any movie with an action hero involves one person saving many people against all odds and, usually all by themselves. You probably have memories of movies that you grew up on, or have watched recently, dancing around in your head right now! These movies make an impression on us. But why? I think it's because we all share the desire to be saved, and see others saved as well. Remember, we are all made in the image of God (Genesis 1:27). So the desire for salvation is woven into our DNA. We love when it is depicted in the movies, television, or books. So let me recommend a book for you to read. It's called "the Bible" and its central figure has been called by many, "the Savior of the world" (1 John 4:14).

I have already covered the gospel of the kingdom of God. However, I want to take a closer look at what this gospel looks like and the mechanics of how it works. But to review, the gospel can be summed up with this (Mark 1:15) and other similar scriptures: "'The time promised by God has come at last!' he announced. 'The Kingdom of God is near! Repent of your sins and believe the Good News!'" Through Jesus Christ, the kingdom of God has been reconciled to mankind! The kingdom of God and God the Creator go hand in hand. More specifically, the kingdom of God is the government of heaven. Mankind needs this government like a fish needs water. But the sin of humans separated us from God and His government. The Good News is that the kingdom of God is available once again, after repentance, if one will believe in Christ as their Lord and Savior.

It's one thing to believe in all of that, and another thing to understand it all. The purpose of this chapter is to literally illustrate the process, operation, or procedure of salvation so that anyone can understand how, and why it works, along with the ability to explain it to somebody else. Below will be my explanation of four simple illustrations that can be used for understanding the gospel message.

The Bridge:

Here we have God and man in communion and harmony with each other, just like at the beginning of creation.

However, due to our past and present sins, we have been separated from God. To be separated from God is a curse that brings with it death upon mankind. Notice the chasm or divide that has been created. If separation from God is a curse of death, then we (mankind) must find a way to get back to Him. There are many ways that people try to accomplish this,

but they actually can be placed into two categories: sin and religion. Either way will get you the same result, death.

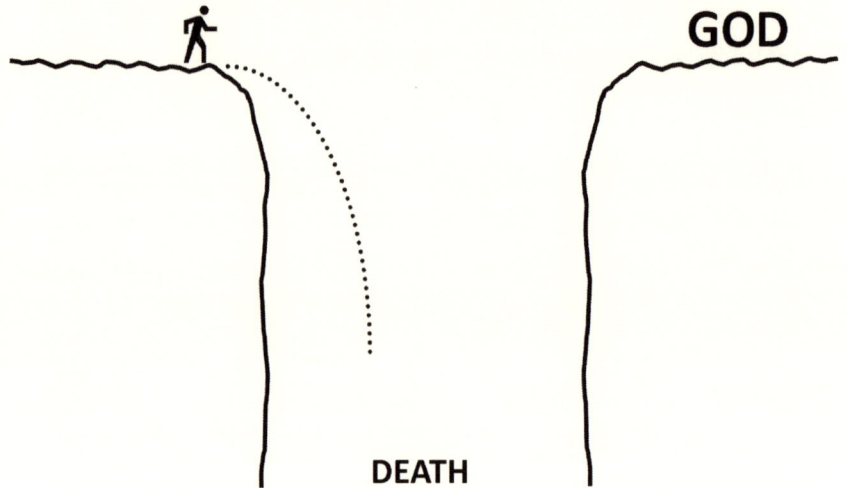

Let me explain. Religion can be defined as anything one
does by their own power to get back to God. This can include,
but is not limited to, worship, being a good person, giving to
the poor, meditating, going to church (or some other religious
building), following rules, sacrifices, praying, chanting, reading sacred scriptures, or anything else one does to please God
or earn rewards. With these efforts, people attempt to cross this
great divide or chasm in order to return to God. However, they
meet their demise at the bottom of the canyon.

Sin is another way man attempts to get to God. Hear me
out! In sin, man tries to make his own rules and provide for
his own needs in life. We choose to get drunk, get high, murder, steal, hate, have sex, lie, fulfill our own desires, cheat, and

otherwise be our own god. In this way we provide for ourselves by making decisions about what we think we need out of life. This way of living becomes what life is all about, being happy and doing whatever you want to do. So, in searching for God, we found ourselves. In other words, our appetites, desires, and how we make sense out of life is defined by us and provided by us. With great effort, our attempts are sadly in vain since our leap of faith is based on the ability of man, which cannot cover the expanse, and leads to destruction.

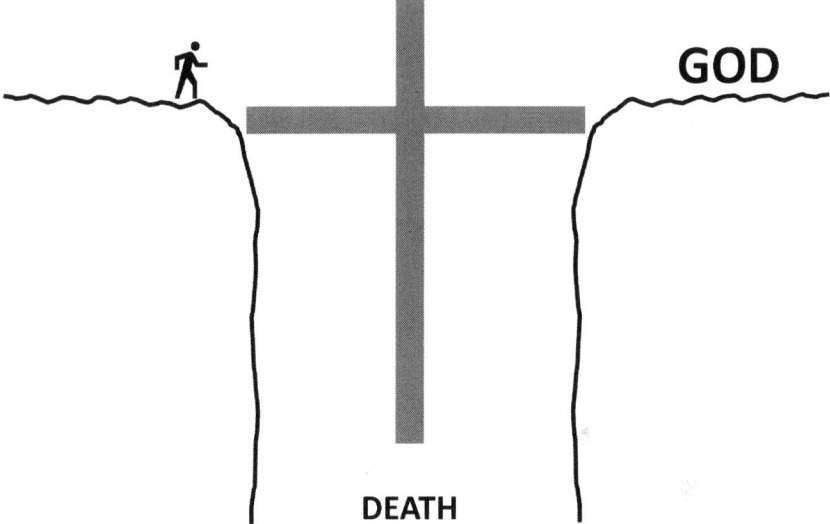

But then Christ our Lord came. His death and resurrection formed a bridge across this space. Here Christ is seen as a bridge, but the Bible calls Him a Mediator (1 Timothy 2:5), or an Advocate (1 John 2:1). In other words, Jesus has negotiated with the Father our way across this gap. We can only assume this offer is contingent upon our acceptance of Jesus Christ as Lord and Savior.

There is a gap between God and man, but Christ has formed a bridge across this gap, and He is the way back to God. Yes, Jesus is the Way, Truth, and Life! No one can get to God unless they go through Jesus Christ first (John 14:6). Titus 3:3-7 sums up this illustration: "Once we, too, were foolish and disobedient. We were misled and became slaves to many lusts and pleasures. Our lives were full of evil and envy, and we hated each other. But—'When God our Savior revealed his kindness and love, he saved us, not because of the righteous things we had done, but because of his mercy. He washed away our sins, giving us a new birth and new life through the Holy Spirit. He generously poured out the Spirit upon us through Jesus Christ our Savior. Because of his grace he declared us righteous and gave us confidence that we will inherit eternal life.'"

The Romans Road:

Here is another way to understand and follow the gospel account and storyline. Use the book of Romans. Using a few select scriptures, one can read through, or easily show someone else, the gospel message which includes how to receive salvation. Side note, these passages can be used with the bridge illustration if you want. Follow along with me in your Bible, or Bible app, as I explain.

First we look at Romans 3:23. Everybody has sinned. That means everyone has missed the mark or standard established in the Garden of Eden by God. In other words, no one is innocent! It does not matter how good of a person you think you are. Your very first wrongful act on this planet placed you in this category. A much more specific passage can be read in Romans 3:10-18. Next we go to Romans 6:23. The only thing that sin pays out is death (remember the bridge illustration). We have not only earned a physical death, but a spiritual death. A spiritual death can be defined as eternal separation from the Father with no further possibilities of mercy or reconciliation. But, we can exchange our eternal damnation for eternal life in Christ Jesus our Lord!

Now we can move on to Romans 5:8. God loves you so much, that even while you were still a rebel against God and His government, an enemy of the state, Christ died for you. Even though you were not deserving, He paid the penalty for your sins that you may be reconciled to God through Christ. Now we can skip to Romans 10:9. This verse details how we accept Jesus and His precious gift. All we have to do is state with our mouth that Jesus is Lord, and that God the Father raised Him from the dead. Upon that confession, which must be an expression of a foundational belief system, you will be saved! Romans 10:13 says it again. Amen! The last stop is at Romans 5:1. Since we have been made right with God and His government by our faith in Christ, we are no longer enemies of God but have found peace with Him through Jesus Christ.

Romans 8:1 explains how God does not condemn anyone who has been reconciled to Him through Christ. FYI... when God condemns someone it is a curse of death! Romans 8:38-39 further explains how the separation between God and man has been reversed through Jesus our King! These are good scriptures to memorize. You can explain the gospel to anyone at any time by memory, or you can have the scriptures listed in your wallet or purse, or you can take a person through the gospel while reading from the Bible. The Romans Road is also a great way to remind yourself of all that Christ has done for you.

Three Turning Points:

Here is an original design that the Lord recently showed me. As with the other illustrations, this is good for personal reflection or sharing the gospel with someone using a simple sheet of scratch paper. One can use this illustration as I propose it or simplify it to suit. We begin with the first point:

God's Design. God's original design is best described in Genesis 1:26-27. Remember that man was given dominion on the planet earth and had direct communion with God as one would with someone at a dinner table. Man was supposed to want what God wants and be what God wanted them to be. Just like a toaster is designed to brown bread on both sides, man was designed to love and obey God while ruling for Him on the planet earth. This is a depiction of the perfect life! However, things went awry at the forbidden tree, turning point #1.

Mankind went down a path of sin and brokenness (Romans 3:23, 3:10). Sin is anything that is against the will of God. Brokenness is the opposite of wholeness. To be whole is to be spiritually healthy and in God's will for your life. To be broken is to be apart from God and His purpose for your life. A continued journey along this path could be labeled as "self-destruction" (Romans 6:23). However, God can cause one to be broken in a good way that will ultimately lead someone closer to God. But, when a person is broken due to sin that is self-destruction since God had no hand in this outcome. At this point most people will choose to "seek change," turning point #2.

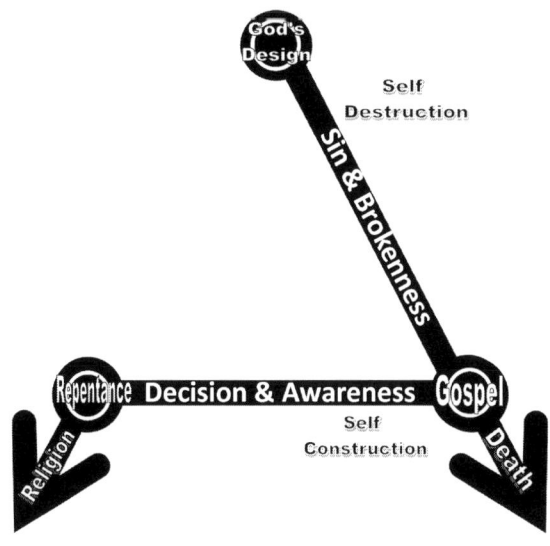

The conscience causes a person to become aware that they are not living the best life possible. Now a decision must be made to change one's life. Most people will find themselves at this place at one point or another. However, not everyone chooses to turn towards God the Creator at this point. There is a whole "self-help" industry for people to consume. Books, DVDs, and seminars are some of the ways that people attempt to "fix themselves." Usually this industry can provide very good information ranging from wisdom and advice, to inspiration and motivation. However, what it cannot change is one's relationship (or lack thereof) with God the Creator. If someone simply maintains this journey of decision and awareness, then they will seek to live a life of good deeds, wisdom, and self-confidence apart from God the Creator. This way of doing things may find great worldly results, but it will not, and cannot, change one's eternal future. There are also many religions out there that claim to teach people how to be a good person. These religions focus on good deeds and meditation. That is why this journey can be best labeled as "self-construction."

The God of creation is the only god that can heal a person's eternal life. The best to hope for in this journey of reflection, awareness, and decision, is that one may find an opportunity to read or hear the gospel! We know that no one can have faith in God or Jesus without hearing the gospel (Romans 10:17). The gospel can lead someone to repentance, and if someone reaches repentance then they will find turning point #3!

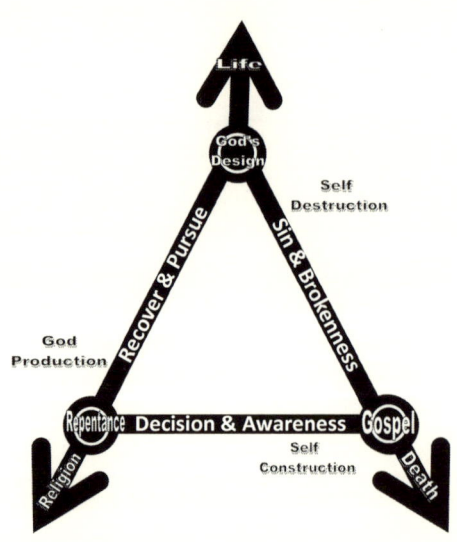

Read all of Romans chapter 10 for greater clarity. I want to focus on Romans 10:9-10 and what repentance actually is to the believer. Repentance is to stop going in one particular direction and turn 180 degrees in the opposite direction. My favorite scripture for explaining how this happens and works is in 2 Chronicles 7:14. Now, let's take a look at Romans 10:9-10. To confess with your mouth means to admit that something is a part of your foundational belief system. In this case, one would be making a confession about the Lord Jesus Christ. To believe that Jesus was raised from the dead is important, since you were not around to witness the event in person. How can someone believe in such a thing? It takes the power of God to change one's mind, especially when it comes to faith. Faith is evidence that something exists even though you cannot see it (Hebrews 11:1). Now, our confession is that Jesus is Lord.

It is very important to understand what a lord is. A lord is a land owner. Land owners own the land and everything on it. You don't believe me? Think about a homeowner. First of all, the bank probably still owns the home, but let's assume the bank has been paid off and the owner has the deed. The "owner" still doesn't fully own the home or the land. Do you know why? They still have to pay taxes on that land. Do you know what happens if they stop paying land taxes? The state or government will seize the land and everything on it, which, obviously, includes the home! That means, in a lot of ways, the state owns you since you are bound to pay or risk losing your rights. Considering this, Jesus is Lord (with a capital "L") over the entire earth! That means He is the real Landowner which means He owns the land and everything on it. The psalmist agrees with me in Psalm 24:1: "The earth is the Lord's, and everything in it. The world and all its people belong to him." So, the confession you are making, is a confession that the Lord owns you, and you will therefore seek His will over your life and attempt to do as He commands you to do. This is so important to understand. Repentance and salvation is more than a prayer. It is a deep rooted foundational belief that JESUS IS LORD! That is why Jesus wanted people to repent and receive the kingdom of God. People who receive the kingdom of God recognize that they do not own anything but they have access to everything since the Lord owns all and will give freely if He desires and it is good for you. WOW! That's worth a praise, right there!

If someone continues along this path, they will recover and pursue. That is, recover from your path apart from God by obeying His instructions for life (2 Timothy 3:16) and healing (1 Peter 2:21-25), and always pursuing God by seeking first His kingdom and righteousness (Matthew 6:33). This path will take you back to God's design by becoming more and more like Jesus the Christ (Romans 8:29). It is important to note that both self-construction and self-destruction ultimately lead to death. However, seeking God's design leads to life. Amen!

Do vs. Done:

This will be the simplest one of the four illustrations to explain. One's understanding of the gospel will go a long way into executing this one since it leaves a ton of room for adlib. First you begin by explaining to someone the difference between religion, which could include Christianity, and faith in Jesus as Lord. Tell them that religion is spelled "**do.**" All of the many world religions (maybe even Christianity, depending on how it is taught) have one thing in common. They all say you have to earn your way back to God and His graces. Religion is about performance (following rules, rituals, duties, etc.). The problem is that one must be perfect in order to get back to the one true God of the Bible. This is impossible since we have all fallen short of perfection (Romans 6:23). No matter how hard one tries, no amount of effort will bring success in returning someone back to God. Therefore, mankind needs a Savior.

Now, the kingdom of God is spelled "**done.**" The gospel, as depicted in the Bible, is not about what mankind can do but what Jesus has done already. The bottom line is, Jesus is our only way back to God. It doesn't matter how hard one tries, destruction is sure to happen unless our lives are built around the Cornerstone (Ephesians 19-21). Anyone's best day is well short of what God demands, which is perfection. Jesus lived that perfect life for us. Through faith, because of Jesus, anyone can be saved since He lived the perfect life. Yes, God wants us to be good people but it won't be good enough for His standards. Anything we do on earth to please God is because we are enabled by God's power to do those things (2 Peter 1:3), not our own power. Ephesians 2:8-9 says it better than I can: "God saved you by his grace when you believed. And you can't take credit for this; it is a gift from God. Salvation is not a reward for the good things we have done, so none of us can boast about it." Be prepared to lead someone to salvation if you can get this far in conversation with them. Otherwise, DO vs DONE is a good way to remind yourself of all Christ has done for you.

THE LOCAL CHURCH

Let's go to church! When someone says that, you know what they are talking about. Most know church as the place where Christians go on Sunday mornings to sing about God and listen to some preaching. Hardcore church goers might even attend on Sunday night and/or Wednesday night. Some are only committed to go to church on Easter and/or Christmas. Ah, yes! Those two times of the year are American past times! We can put on our Sunday's best, sing a little tune, dance a little jig, and be home before the biscuits burn. After all, a service on Easter or Christmas will normally amount to something along the lines of a commercial add as the church puts on their best face that seems to say, "Please come back to church again!" Other than that, church is a gathering place where acquaintances and friends are met and we, overall, feel a sense of belonging to a club type of setting. You might even be able to play basketball, workout, drink cappuccinos, and lounge in a facility known as the, "Family Center." That way, there's no need to go to any other places. Furthermore, the churches we usually choose from have people that go there who probably look, dress, and act the way we do. That way, we will not have to feel uncomfortable because that is what it's all about! And, when things do not go our way and we get upset or unhappy, all we have to do is pick from any of the hundreds of churches in the community to grace our presence with. They should feel lucky to have us, right?

You may be saying, "I don't want to go to church!" There are many reasons why this might be. The first and most likely reason has to do with injury, or what can be called "church hurt." That means you were somehow mistreated by the staff or normal church goers. If that happens multiple times at different churches then someone may decide to stay at home for good.

The second reason might be that you do not feel welcome. This is probably because you have attended churches where you are very different from the regular attendees that go there. Maybe you are a different race, have tattoos or piercings, don't dress "properly," or anything else that would make you stand out in a negative manner.

Third, maybe you feel like church is where hypocrites go. That means you have noticed, all too often, people in churches who don't practice what they preach. A fourth reason is that sometimes churches seem too needy or that they are always asking for money. You are expected to give every time you walk in the building, not to mention all of the extra projects that need to be funded. You were led to believe that giving to the church is like giving to God but, somehow, that has worn thin.

Fifth, maybe there is too much conflict within the church. Backbiting, gossip, and control can be major issues amongst the people. Sixth, it's the same old thing every single Sunday! Once a church finds a routine that works, they rarely deviate from it. Finally, even though Jesus is a pretty cool guy, church just seems irrelevant to your day to day life. It teaches sound biblical doctrine but the sermons provide no practical help to your life.

To church or not to church, that is the question. Which is better: to commune with the people of God at one of the most established institutions in world history or go "Lone Ranger," just you and God? It is a tough decision. Before you decide, it is important to know all of the facts. One needs to know what church is and what it is not. What exactly did Jesus and the apostles set in motion in the first century and are we still practicing that program today? Is church necessary? What are all the rituals and ceremonies about? Hopefully the truth will enlighten your mind and lead you to join church for what it is instead of reject it for what it is not!

The First Century Church:

The very beginning of the church does not resemble what we know and see today at all! Back then, new people were join-ing the church in droves. The first sermon ever preached for the church brought in 3000 new people that very day (Acts 2:41). Mathematicians would call that "exponential growth." For instance, AD 100 saw maybe as little as 25,000 people linked to the church. But in AD 310, as much as 20 million Christians had joined. For that to happen, the church has to add over 95,000 brand new people who have found salvation in Christ a year. These, of course, would not be church transfers but newly saved people. I like to describe these folks as being "fresh off the boat" in comparison to those who would sail to the New World, America, like in Christopher Columbus's time and even before then. If the church was still experiencing such massive growth, every church, on every corner would be standing room only on Sundays! This is obviously not the case. If it were, the streets would be empty and all or most businesses would be closed.

How did the church grow so fast in ancient times? First, Christianity was largely an illegal religion throughout the world. This brought about persecution and even death to those who would claim allegiance to Christ. Second, they did not have church buildings built that could be solely dedicated to the gathering of all these people. People mainly met in houses during this time. In fact, each church house did not have an individual name like churches do today. For example, every church house in Corinth was considered to be the church of Corinth. Third, they did not have the Bible as we have it today. Of course they had Old Testament scriptures but they were illegal documents that had to be passed around from group to group. Also, the gospels and letters from the apostles were still being written at the time. It was the apostles' job to train everyone regarding what they needed to know about Christ. Fourth, there was not any professional form of church leadership. The church did have leaders, but they were not formally trained by any institutional organization like they are today. Fifth, none of the things we can see in church today existed at all. There were no bands, pulpits, pews, or nurseries. And sixth, the church was hard to join back then. There was some kind of probationary period so the new people could prove they were worthy to be a part of the church; that is, people needed to see certain proofs that you were indeed saved by Christ.

What does all of this have to do with church growth in the first century? The full answer is way too broad for me to tackle in this book. What I will say is that it has something to do with persecution. History tells us that whenever and wherever the church is persecuted, it will grow at a rapid rate. There are many reasons for this. What we do know is that the church is not being persecuted in western society today. When the church is not persecuted, it builds buildings, hires college trained preachers, invents programs, writes bylaws, uses music bands, and other stuff. All of that seems very natural but it stunts the growth of the church overall. Entire books have been written on this subject. Let me prove what I am saying by using one last example.

Christians in China grew from about 2 million in 1949 to about 60 million in the late 70s to early 80s. That means that over 2.14 million brand new people had to join every year. The success of the church in China is largely due to an underground church that sprang up during the reign of Mao Zedong. He launched the "Cultural Revolution" going on at the time. One of its aims was to eliminate Christianity from China. Missionaries were banished from the country in 1953 but were allowed back, along with church officials, in the early 80s. Obviously, they expected to find the church wiped out and weakened. But it had grown beyond anyone's wildest imagination. This all happened when the people had very few Bibles. They often had to tear pages out of one Bible and then pass those pages around from house to house. Of course, there were no professional clergy or central organization. There were no large gatherings. But, that Chinese movement grew exponentially.

Christendom:

So how did we get to the mode of church that we know today? To understand that, we must go all the way back to 313 AD and the Edict of Milan. This is when the church shifted from being a movement that takes place in the margins of society, to one that is a centralized institution. A newly crowned emperor, Constantine, claimed that he had a conversion experience to Christianity so he made Christianity the official state religion to the exclusion of all others. Furthermore, Constantine joined church and state together. Therefore he needed all the church leaders to come up with a common theology, or orthodoxy, which would unite all of the Christians within the empire. Then Constantine created a centralized church organization, based in Rome, to command the churches and Christians all over the world. Politics between church and state were created and still apply today. The Roman Empire officially began to tolerate the Christian movement. Christians were given legal rights which included the right to organize.

Many changes within the church happened due to the Edict of Milan. Some I have already mentioned but here are some more. First, infant baptism became a way to guarantee salvation for a baby. Second, Sunday became the official day of rest and church attendance. Third, huge church buildings and large congregations became the norm. Fourth, as a professional clergy gained more and more power, the laity or regular folk became more and more passive. Fifth, tithing became a system to fund the institution and increase its wealth. Sixth, the word "church" started being used to describe the building rather than the gathering of the saints. And seventh, the use of the Old Testament, rather than the New Testament was used to support these changes and many others.

Maybe the greatest change that Constantine brought about is the church changing from a missional, "send them out" movement, to an attractional, "bring them in" movement. In other words, instead of leading people to be changed from within and then sending them out to make disciples, the church would bring people in, and change their outward appearance (clothes, speech, friends, personality, etc.). Upon this change, their inward change could then be assumed to have taken place and the church maintained wealth and political power.

The Renaissance and the Reformation weakened this mode of church (14-16 centuries). The church lost most, or all, of its dominance during the Enlightenment period (19-20 centuries). It helped to bring about the separation between church and state. The Enlightenment established reason, through philosophy and science, over revelation from God. Philosophy and science would become the new mediator of truth. Therefore, the church's message became marginalized, just like in the first century. But, there was a major problem. The church kept on, and still is functioning as if it is still the center of society! So there are two issues here. Christendom severely stunted the growth of the church as it was experiencing it in the first century, but the church did succeed in what was important to it at the time. However, now that the church was no longer the center of society, it could not accomplish and succeed in the way that it did before. Christendom is fundamentally different from the first century church, which was a grassroots movement made up of a network of communities. Now the church has lost its exponential growth potential, along with its societal and political power or influence. In that sense, Christendom is dead. We are now in the post-Christendom (post Christian) era. That means the loss of the primacy of the Christian worldview in political affairs in favor of other worldviews like secularism or nationalism. In other words, the glory days of the church are over.

The Church:

When we say, "Let's go to church," we are talking about a building, but this is not the biblical definition of church. *Ekklesia* is the original Greek word used in the Bible that has been translated into the English word "church." It can be defined as "an assembly" or, "called out ones." Therefore, "church," refers to the people and not the building. Romans 16:5 says, "Also give my greetings to the church that meets in their home." So the church is a gathering of people who have been called out for the Lord's purposes.

Ephesians 1:22-23 reads: "God has put all things under the authority of Christ and has made him head over all things for the benefit of the church. And the church is his body, it is made full and complete by Christ, who fills all things everywhere with himself." We can see that another definition of "church" is, "the body of Christ." Think about this in the literal sense for a second. The Bible says that "Christ is the head of the church" (Ephesians 5:23). So, Christ is the head or authority of a body. Just as your head controls your body, so Christ, ideally, controls the church. At least that is the way it is supposed to be but all too often, churches are controlled by one Senior Pastor who claims to be operating the church in the exact way that Christ is leading him to. Everyone is left to assume that this is taking place, and will rarely challenge the Senior Pastor on his obedience to Christ, or the biblical backing for his operations.

Churches everywhere are using mere mortals to build their churches instead of letting Jesus do it. This is one of the greatest sins of the church today. "How can Jesus build a church while seated in heaven" you ask? A church is not built with bricks and mortar but upon Christ who is the chief cornerstone (Ephesians 2:19-21). It is built on the revelation that Jesus is the Christ or Messiah (Matthew 16:13-18). Take note of Matthew 16:18. We can see that Jesus is not only the chief cornerstone of the church but also the architect. The church is to be submissive to Christ and that means judging yourself based on your obedience to Christ and not by man-made or earthly measurements that all too often lead us in the wrong direction.

One good way to discern if the Lord is leading you is if you are making decisions based on what Christ wants, even when that is not what you want. Total submission to Christ means doing things that are not pleasing to you in order to please Christ.

The church is representative of two groups of people. Everyone, everywhere, all around the earth who have a personal relationship with Christ is often referred to as the "universal church." This term is not in the Bible. It was created by Catholics who believe that the Pope governs Christians all over the world. But, much like "rapture" and "trinity," which are not in the Bible either, the term "universal church" still describes a real thing. 1 Corinthians 12:13 says, "Some of us are Jews, some are Gentiles, some are slaves, and some are free. But we have all been baptized into one body by one Spirit, and we all share the same Spirit." Those who have the Holy Spirit in them belong to God (Romans 8:9) and the purpose of Christ is to not only die for one nation but to unite all of the people of God who are scattered all around the earth (John 11:51-52).

Next, we have the local church. In Galatians 1:1-2 we can see Paul referring to the churches of Galatia. So we have local churches, which we pass everyday as we are out and about, that do not represent all of the people of God around the world. They are a smaller local body meant for God's purposes on a local level. The idea is that those who are raised on a local level will later be sent out to serve or disciple other areas of the city, state, country, or world.

A Gathering Community:

We have discussed two different church eras. One was in the first century while the other, Christendom, began in the third century. They can be compared to house churches and traditional institutional churches of today, respectively. House churches will be harder to find without being invited by someone who attends. Traditional churches, of course, can be found very easily by anyone who wants to look. Either way, or in spite of the things I have mentioned about the local church up to this point, attending a church somewhere is very necessary. Some people cannot make it to church due to health, transportation, or occupational reasons. However, I pray that you will find a church that will come to you or offer live viewing via the internet. One's salvation does not depend on church attendance. It depends on Christ. But let me ask you this: How can someone depend on Christ without depending on the body that is attached to Christ?

There are many reasons to attend church. I will discuss a few of them here. First, you should show up and worship with the people of God. This can also be called corporate worship. I will discuss and define worship a little later but let me say for now, worship of a Holy and righteous God is not only an individual sport but also a team sport. The game of basketball can be played one-on-one and on up to five-on-five. No one would claim that basketball is meant to be a one-on-one sport only. In fact, the brilliance of the game can be better regarded during a five-on-five matchup. Worship is the same way. Individual worship is necessary but worship amongst your brothers and sisters in Christ is just as necessary.

Second, it is important and vital to hear the teaching and preaching of the word of God. 2 Timothy 4:2 says, "Preach the word of God. Be prepared, whether the time is favorable or not. Patiently correct, rebuke, and encourage your people with good teaching." We are told to do this but we must also hear it.

1 Timothy 4:6 tells us to be "trained in the words of the faith and of the good doctrine that you have followed" (ESV). So we must be trained in the word of God before we go and preach it. We also know that "All Scripture is inspired by God and is useful to teach us what is true and to make us realize what is wrong in our lives. It corrects us when we are wrong and teaches us to do what is right" (2 Timothy 3:16). Listening to nationally syndicated preachers is okay, but their messages to you are not designed to overtake or replace teaching and preaching on a local level. You need people who will not only teach you the word of God but will hold you accountable to it.

Third, you need a sense of belonging to something much bigger than yourself. Upon your salvation, it is not you against the world. It is the church against the world. You must join the people to be a part of the movement of God on the earth. Also, you need to feel other people's joy and pain. That will remind you that your problems can always be trumped by someone else. Furthermore, rejoicing with someone during their joyous moments will teach you unselfishness and how not to covet what you neighbor has obtained. Over all, mankind has always needed to feel a part of a larger group. That is why people love to attend sporting events where most everyone is rooting for the same team. That is why we have feelings of patriotism. That is why we join book clubs. The movement of God on the earth is about you, but it is not all about you. It's about other people too. It is time that you get to know some of them, pray for them, and love them.

Fourth, God can speak to you at church. It is true that God can speak to you anywhere and anytime. However, the church environment (more specifically, the assembly of the people of God) can produce a tangible anointing that you might feel on your body, emotions, and/or mind. Worshipping with the people of God can open up your mind and heart to receive from God in such a way that you may not be able to receive alone. God can speak to you during corporate worship, the teaching and preaching, others praying for you, or through a conversation with another brother/sister during service. The closer you get to the people of God, the closer you will get to God, and the better God can communicate with you.

Fifth, the people of God can uplift and support you during your walk with Christ. Proverbs 27:17 says, "As iron sharpens iron, so a friend sharpens a friend." It takes a person of God to edify; that is, instruct or improve on a moral or intellectual basis, another person of God. This can be done through mentorship. Whether formally or informally, someone may take it upon themselves to mentor, or disciple, you. You may do that for someone else too. In this way, and others, we might find someone to lean on and that can lean on us. Galatians 6:2-3 says, "Share each other's burdens, and in this way obey the law of Christ. If you think you are too important to help someone, you are only fooling yourself. You are not that important." Those are strong words! We should obey them.

Sixth, church provides a place to exercise your spiritual and natural gifts. Read 1 Corinthians chapter 12 for very good clarity. 1 Corinthians 12:7 says, "A spiritual gift is given to each of us so we can help each other." So, the reason that God gives the people of the church spiritual gifts, is so they can use them to help each other out within community. These gifts can include but are not limited to wise advice, faith, healing, special knowledge, miracles, prophesy, and many more! Just as the human body has many parts, so does the body of Christ. All of these many parts combine to make up one body. Each part has a gift that the body needs to live an abundant life. The eyes need the feet. The feet need the hands. The hands need the brain etc. How can any part function without the stomach which can turn food into energy? Church can give you a place to exercise these gifts that you have. Just like the body needs exercise to maintain health and get stronger, so do you. Flex your gifts and they will grow and strengthen for the glory of God!

Seventh, church provides a place where you can enlist and start serving the community. The gifts that we have are not only to serve the church family but also the community at large. Many places in the Bible talk about serving others. Jesus did a really good job of it in Matthew chapter 25. Here He uses a parable to explain some things to those who were listening. Read the whole chapter and you will be blessed! During the parable, the Lord is telling His listeners to feed the hungry, give the thirsty a drink, clothe the naked, care for the sick, and visit the imprisoned. As we do for these people, we are doing for Christ. That is how He sees it! If you help another, you are helping the Lord. But if you shun someone, it is like you are shunning the Lord! Take heed, there can be eternal consequences for that! Sure, you can do this without joining a church family but, more than likely, most of you are not serving the community at all. Giving to charities is great and is sometimes the best way to help a segment of society, but it is important that we serve with our hands too. Jesus came to serve (Mark 10:45, Matthew 20:28). He even washed the feet of His disciples (John 13:1-17). Jesus also served evil tax collectors (Luke 19:1-10), prostitutes (John 8:1-11), and those who would murder Him (Luke 22:47-51). Serve the community and the Lord will bless you for it.

Eighth, the Lord wants us to meet together on a regular basis. Hebrews 10:25 says, "And let us not neglect our meeting together, as some people do, but encourage one another, especially now that the day of his return is drawing near." It is important to note that, back in the first century when this letter was written, some people were neglecting to meet together, not because they were lazy or did not want to, but because they were frightened for their life! Remember, Christians were being persecuted within the Roman Empire at the time. However, here in western society, we are free to meet and worship together as much as we want. So, if those who were frightened for their life were told to continue to meet with one another, then I know that we should.

If you have the spirit of God in you, then you are saved or have been given salvation through Christ. That makes you a part of the universal church, or those people of God all around the world. But to say or think that you are part of a greater community without being a part of a smaller community does not make any sense. How can someone be a citizen of the greater Chicago area without being a part of a smaller Chicago area? It does not seem logical. Meanwhile, every letter in the New Testament is written to churches and assumes that all Christians in the area are a member of those churches. So, if you lived back in the first century and did not belong to a local church body, then those letters would not have been written with you in mind. That is worth considering. Again, church membership is not necessary for salvation but should we be doing the least amount possible to inherit the kingdom of God? The whole Bible is written to the children of God, who have been justified by faith, and are called "the church." It only makes sense. Join a traditional church or home church today!

The Sacraments and More:

I have explained before, one of the major hindrances to the movement of God is the word "church" being associated with a building instead of a people who can gather anywhere.

Furthermore, these buildings are considered sacred places. "Sacred" means to be connected with God or dedicated to religious purposes and deserving of reverence and respect. However, this is an Old Testament way of thinking! In other words, it is an outdated way of thinking. What I mean is, the only reason why a church space should be considered sacred is if God's Holy Spirit is present (tangibly speaking since God is everywhere). The only way that could happen is if two or more people are gathered in the name or authority of the Lord Jesus Christ (Matthew 18:20). So, it is not the building that is sacred but the Holy Spirit within the people of God.

I do not have enough space here to go into a thorough exposition of the Holy Temple of God, the tabernacle, and the Ark of the Covenant. These are very important Old Testament things. The Temple and tabernacle were considered holy and sacred back then for good reason since God's presence was there. More specifically, God's presence was located on the Mercy Seat as a part of the Ark of the Covenant. The Ark of the Covenant was mobile and could be moved. Therefore, wherever the Ark was, God's presence was there as well. Also, God gave very specific instructions on how to build the Ark of the Covenant, the tabernacle, and the Temple. That makes them sacred as well since God was, literally, the architect of all of them. A priest had to be used to atone for the sins of the people by sprinkling blood on the Mercy Seat, among other very specific things. These very specific things were all detailed and instituted by God. Therefore, God created the need for priests, rituals, ceremonies, and sacraments. However, these were no longer needed once Christ came, since He is God in the flesh.

God no longer kept his spirit confined to the Temple so there would be no need to meet Him there. God made sure there would be no confusion by allowing Israel to lose possession of the Ark of the Covenant during their exile to Babylon. Now the human body is the temple of the Holy Spirit (1 Corinthians 6:19-20) however, only those who are saved have the Holy Spirit (Romans 8:9). So, there is no longer a need for a sacred temple. In fact, it's our bodies that are supposed to be seen as sacred! Why? Because the Holy Spirit resides there. Yet, we still see buildings as sacred or special religious places even though the only thing that makes those spaces sacred, is the Holy Spirit within the people who are gathered there at the time. Furthermore, we think that the events that happen inside the church building are sacred as well since they are taking place inside of a sacred building. Now, let's discuss some of the things that take place inside of the church building. Why does the church do these things? What do these sacraments or dedications mean? It is time to dissect a church service.

Worship:

Most people typically think of worship as singing to or about God or Jesus. Church services, usually, start with singing at the beginning of service. The worship leaders are supposed to lead everyone into worship while they sing and the congregation can follow their lead. However, singing to God and playing instruments are just a couple of forms of worship. It is actually a state of mind and a state of heart. *Proskuneo*, the original Greek word translated into "worship", means "to fall down before" or "bow down before" a person or object. So, we are to bow down before the King of the universe. It does not have to happen literally. It should be done in everything we do and everywhere we are. Some people think we should only worship in sacred places (John 4:20). Jesus changed all of that with His coming (John 4:21). He said "true worshipers will worship the Father in spirit and in truth" (John 4:23) because God is a spirit. To worship in spirit, we must be born again to receive the Holy Spirit, without which one cannot worship in spirit.

To worship in truth, one must respond to the truth that has been heard and read in the Bible by giving reverence and glory to God. This can be through singing, dancing, thinking, praying, or reading the Bible. But, it can also be done through bowling, working, cutting the grass, painting, or anything else! The Bible says, "So whether you eat or drink, or whatever you do, do it all for the glory of God." (1 Corinthians 10:31). It also says, "And whatever you do or say, do it as a representative of the Lord Jesus, giving thanks through him to God the Father" (Colossians 3:17). Even though the Lord loves singing, dancing, and playing instruments, His favorite form of worship is for you to give yourself completely over to Him in every way, every day. Paul explains this well in Romans 12:1: "I plead with you to give your bodies to God because of all he has done for you. Let them be a living and holy sacrifice-the kind he will find acceptable. This is truly the way to worship him." Worship is a sacrifice! But with God's spirit in us, we can sacrifice our total body, heart and mind, to the glory of God!

Preaching:

The people we normally hear preaching is the Senior Pastor or some other subservient pastor. These people are often trained in some type of Bible school or college. Some even go to seminary to obtain their doctorate degree. I am quite sure that most preachers are good at what they do and are fully qualified to be in that position. However, anyone who has been saved by Christ, discipled by those mature in the faith, and have explored the Bible is qualified as well. Israel used to need a priest or prophet to communicate with God for them. But, because of what Jesus has done for us that has completely changed! All of God's people are considered "royal priests" (1 Peter 2:9), "holy priests" (1 Peter 2:5), "a Kingdom of priests" (Revelation 1:6), and "priests of God and of Christ" (Revelation 20:6). We are all called to preach or teach in some form or fashion, maybe not from a pulpit, but within your everyday life. In fact, any pastor or preacher should allow his congregation to challenge him (in an honorable and respectful manner) based on the word of God. Why? It is because we are all priests!

The Altar:

In the Old Testament, an altar is any structure upon which offerings or sacrifices are made. Basically, it is a place where someone gives a possession of great value up to God. Long ago, one could take their best animal or crop and burn it up on an altar. The idea is to give God something you find valuable or important to let God know that you find Him even more valuable and important. This was commanded by God for centuries. Now, however, we know an altar as the front of the church where we can go to pray, get prayed over, or give our lives to Jesus. That's okay since, in a broad sense, an altar is any place where a person can give their self away to God in some manner. However, it must be known that every human heart has an altar on the inside. That is where the decision to lay one's life down before God can take place. You may like a physical place like the front of a church service, a garden, a prayer room, or in your car but anywhere your heart is, a potential altar is as well. Anytime we surrender control over a particular aspect of our life and give it to God, it's like we are laying that thing down on an altar and burning it up, giving it to God to let Him deal with it!

Anointing:

Many churches will pray for people by laying hands on them and anointing (or smearing) them with oil, usually on the forehead. This was done many times in the Old Testament to the high priest and his descendants as well as the furnishings in the tabernacle to mark them as holy. Anointing in the New Testament is a bit vague but we can see people healing the sick with anointing oil (Mark 6:13, James 5:13). Anointing with oil is not a magic trick, and there is nothing in the Bible to suggest that anointing oil possesses special powers. Neither does the Bible command us to use anointing oil. It does not forbid it either. Furthermore, Christians may be given an anointing from God. This does not mean oil is used, but that God has smeared, or empowered, blessed, or protected His servant for a particular task. In this manner, any Christian who is willing to serve God will be anointed in some way.

Communion:

Maybe you have attended a church on a day when they serve communion. A couple of trays are usually passed around with grape juice and wafers on them. This is normally a ritualistic and formal ceremony. It was not that way originally. At first, it was simply a meal between friends, Jesus and His disciples having a Passover celebration. Communion is now known primarily as the "Last Supper" due to Leonardo da Vinci's famous painting. To fully understand, one has to go back and study the story of the Passover (Exodus 12). That is when God sent death into the land of Egypt but allowed death to pass over any house which had the blood of a slaughtered lamb smeared on the door post. Jesus would become the last slaughtered lamb for all eternity. He wanted the disciples to remember Him and His sacrifice.

Jesus explained that the bread they were eating represented His body which would be broken. The men broke the bread and ate it. Then Jesus said the wine represents His blood that would spill out upon death. It would be a bitter cup for Jesus to drink (Matthew 26:39). The men drank the wine. Jesus wanted the disciples to do this often during their meals with one another. Therefore, Christian Communion was never meant to be a religious ceremony. It was to take place during a real meal with real food. This ceremony would work much better during a church banquet or picnic. Better yet, families can do this at home, or with friends during a meal! You can open the Bible and read the biblical account or just speak from the heart as you all remember what Christ did for you. It's that easy. As for Church services, there is nothing wrong with how it has been done. Just know the origins behind it and do it on your own during real meals. The story of the Lord's Supper can be found in Matthew 26, Mark 14, Luke 22, and John 13.

Giving:

I believe that anyone who attends church regularly should also be regularly giving to that church. It makes sense when you stop being selfish and think about it. Churches are supposed to be non-profit organizations (traditionally speaking). If no one gives money then how will the lights, maintenance, staff, insurance, and community service be funded? Why should anyone reap the benefits of such service without paying into it? We have cable subscriptions, magazine subscriptions, and exercise memberships. Shouldn't we pay into church, which is for the Lord's work as well?

Almost all churches (I want to say every church) teach tithing incorrectly. First of all, tithing is an Old Testament concept. The Israelites were required, by God's law, to give 10 percent of their crops and livestock to the temple or tabernacle (Leviticus 27, Numbers 18, Deuteronomy 14, and 2 Chronicles 31). Furthermore, there were even more tithes to give for various reasons, pushing the percentage total to over 23 percent. Anyway, Jesus' death and resurrection brought us into what we call the New Testament (covenant, agreement). Nowhere in the New Testament is it commanded or suggested for people to tithe in a legalistic or systematic fashion. The New Testament does mention the importance and benefits of giving joyfully. 10 percent is not mentioned but we are to give as we are able to (1 Corinthians 16:2). Overall, tithing is not a command from God but giving joyfully and regularly is, whether that giving be to the church or something/someone else. It is important to pray about how much to give (2 Corinthians 9:7). Ask for the Holy Spirit to check your heart. Selfishness and greed may be found there.

Here is my personal take on tithing and giving. I recommend that all Christians tithe. It is an Old Testament concept that still works today. First, tithing is a good way to simplify your giving regimen. I don't want to offend but we are all selfish and greedy on some level or another. Let's be honest. If we leave it to ourselves to decide each and every time when and how much to give then we will, more than likely, give a lot less than we should. So, in this way, I see tithing as a baseline minimum. Second, giving will lead to your provision. Jesus said, "Give, and you will receive. Your gift will return to you in full-pressed down, shaken together to make room for more, running over, and poured into your lap. The amount you give will determine the amount you get back" (Luke 6:38). Therefore, giving and prosperity are linked together. It is important to note that God will always give back much more than you put in.

All you money investors out there…there is no money vehicle that is better than the kingdom of God and His financial system! But, God is not limited to return your investment monetarily. He can choose to provide in many other ways instead. I could give several examples of how money, protection, provision, or something else came my way just when I needed it. In fact, I am so confident in giving (and my tithe keeps me consistent) that I rarely worry about money or provision. I just assume it will be there just when I need it. It always is!

Sabbath:

Why do the vast majority of churches meet on Sundays? God instituted a day of rest, called the Sabbath, for Israel in the Old Testament (Exodus 31, Deuteronomy 5). It would take place on the seventh day, Saturday. This would be a day where no one was allowed to work. The people were commanded to observe this day or be put to death as punishment. There were also commands given about having a sacred assembly, "a holy convocation." The New Testament records Jews meeting in synagogues on the Sabbath as well.

Some people say that Constantine changed the Sabbath from Saturday to Sunday in 321 A.D. But this is not true. All he did was institute a day of rest for Rome. The church adopted Sundays as a day of worship in the first century (Acts 20:7, 1 Corinthians 16:2). The church began meeting on Sundays, probably because Jesus was risen from the dead on that day. The Sabbath day did not change, though. In fact, there is no command to the church to observe a Sabbath day, whether on Saturday or Sunday (Colossians 2:14-17, Romans 14:5-6). The day a church chooses to worship together is irrelevant. The early church met every day (Acts 2:46-47).

A Sabbath day is no longer necessary. The people of God do not find rest on a particular day anymore. Our rest is found in Jesus Christ (Matthew 11:28, Hebrews 4:9-11). First, there is no more labor needed to keep the Mosaic Law and please

God. Second, God sanctified and made the Sabbath holy but Jesus makes us and everyday holy. Third, Jesus is the Lord of the Sabbath and did not observe it all the time while living on earth (Matthew 12). Now, there is no other Sabbath rest except for in Christ.

Baby Dedications:

Constantine made religious changes in Rome in 321 A.D. Those changes led to Catholicism. One of the seven sacraments of the Catholic Church is "confirmation." The child, supposedly, receives the gift of the Holy Spirit after being anointed on the forehead by a bishop. This is ludicrous since each person must make an individual choice to accept Jesus as Lord of their life. Only then can someone receive the Holy Spirit. This cannot be done by someone's anointing oil or blessing. Now some churches do a watered down version of that called a baby dedication. It is a way to dedicate your child to the Lord. There is nothing wrong with this ceremony but it will not dedicate the child to the Lord by itself. The child's parents or guardians must pray for them daily and model a life of living for Christ. A child dedication is a daily process. No one prayer, or ceremony, can change that.

Heaven:

Over the years, the church has really watered down the gospel message. Most believe the gospel is that Jesus died for your sins so you can go to heaven. This may be true but it is not the gospel. The Bible is not about going to heaven. So, a lot of Christians live a life where heaven is the main goal to achieve. This is a faulty view. A person's place in heaven has been earned by Christ. There is nothing to achieve. Upon a person's salvation, their eternal future has been taken care of. With that being said, the Bible is about how to live on the planet earth under submission to God or Christ. Salvation is not about heaven as much as it is about coming into fellowship with God.

Heaven is a benefit of that and is included in the deal, along with other things. When people live a life for heaven then the things they do for God are about getting to that goal. God wants you to do what He wants for no other reason than you love Him more than you love yourself. In that way, heaven is not the goal. Pleasing God is! When Christians learn about God's grace, and how one can still make it to heaven even though they still sin, then they can lose their motivation to stop sinning and conforming to the image of Christ (Romans 8:29). This has created a dilemma that can be expressed in the question, "Are we saved to sin?" In other words, why stop sinning when God's grace will cover the sin and still allow one to go to heaven? If heaven is the goal, and one can get there without putting to death the deeds of the body (Romans 8:13), then why do it? If Christ has died for our past, present, and future sins then why change?

The real gospel should be taught more often. This includes our separation from God due to all the bad things that we do, our reconciliation to God through Jesus Christ in spite of our sins, and us living our lives on the earth in response to the wonderful gift that has been given to us. If heaven was the main goal then it would be better that we die right after our salvation because then we would immediately go to heaven and be free from suffering and sin. Paul was honest when he admitted that he had a desire to die and go be with Christ (Philippians 1:21-25) but he recognized that was a selfish desire. God had more work for him to do on earth. He knew the Lord would keep him alive to benefit all the people he was called to help and raise up in Christ. So, the gospel is not about heaven. It is about how we live our lives on earth for God. Of course, heaven is a great hope for us all, especially those on their death bed. It's just not the purpose of life.

Baptism:

Baptism means, literally, to be submerged into something. Most know baptism as a ceremony when someone is lowered down into water and brought back up again. Churches can perform this event on site, at a lake, or a pool. Some churches misinterpret certain scriptures and teach that water baptism is necessary for salvation. That is not true! The thief, who was crucified next to Jesus, finding salvation without water baptism should prove that.

There are two types of baptism: a physical or water baptism and a spiritual baptism. The water baptism is a literal event while a spiritual baptism is a figurative event. Paul talks about there being only one baptism in Ephesians 4:5. Some people are confused by this. All that Paul wanted to express in this passage was that no matter the differences between Christians, they all serve the same Lord and have the same faith. When he said one baptism, he was either referring to the water baptism or the spiritual baptism. Reading further in the chapter, we can see that Paul wanted the people to be unified amongst each other, focusing on their common points rather than where they were different.

John the Baptist spoke about both types of baptisms. He said, "I baptize you with water; but someone is coming soon who is greater than I am-so much greater that I'm not even worthy to be his slave and untie the straps of his sandals. He will baptize you with the Holy Spirit and with fire" (Luke 3:16). No one knew what he was talking about at the time but they would soon learn about spiritual baptism as we can see in Acts 1:8 and Acts 2. Spiritual baptism is when one receives the Holy Spirit and becomes saved by Christ (Romans 8:9). You can receive the Holy Spirit, "If you confess with your mouth that Jesus is Lord and believe in your heart that God raised him from the dead, you will be saved" (Romans 10:9). Remember, whoever is saved has been gifted with the Holy Spirit.

Water baptism is a reenactment of the more important process of spiritual baptism. It is the means by which a person can make a public confession of faith in Christ. The person has already died to him or herself and has been made a new creation through Christ (2 Corinthians 5:17). This has been done invisibly so, a way to show the world what has happened in the spirit or invisible realm is to partake in water baptism. This reenactment is a way of announcing what has already happened on the inside of you; that is, your sinful nature has been put to death. Therefore, you participate in water baptism, "For you were buried with Christ when you were baptized. And with him you were raised to new life because you trusted the mighty power of God, who raised Christ from the dead." (Colossians 2:12). Lowering you into the water is imagery for lowering you into your grave. As you are raised out of the water, it is like you being brought back to life, or brought out of the grave, through Christ's work.

If water baptism is not necessary for salvation then should we do it? Absolutely! First, the Bible mentions many times about being baptized by water. God expects you to do it. In the first century, it was expected for anyone who confessed Jesus to get baptized by water ASAP. If anyone would have refused to do that, their salvation or conversion would have been brought into question. Back then, being baptized in public was dangerous because you would then be associated with Jesus and Christianity which was illegal and punishable by death. Therefore, only a true convert would even think or agree to do something like that. Secondly, Jesus, your Lord and Savior, was baptized (Luke 3:21-22)! This is enough of a reason since anyone who believes in Jesus should always want to follow in His footsteps.

THE GREAT COMMISSION

There has been quite a bit of information covered in this book so far. We discussed the unfiltered gospel of the kingdom of God as preached by Jesus and His apostles. The true gospel must be preached so anyone who hears will know what they are getting into when they decide to call Jesus their Lord. We talked about prayer and how it appropriates the benefits of the kingdom of God for your life, which includes a relationship and communion with the King of the universe, provision for anything that you need, and protection from anyone or anything against you. There is no such thing as being a follower of Jesus if you do not pray, period.

We talked about the Bible and how it came from original writings that are inerrant or without errors and contradictions. It is also infallible; that is, trustworthy and reliable since it contains no defects. In other words, you should believe and obey the entirety of the scriptures. We talked about God who embodies the Trinity which includes the Father, the Son, and the Holy Spirit. All three are distinct personalities who are God. Yet, there is only one God. We also discussed the person of Christ who is the Son, Jesus. Jesus is 100% God and 100% human. He is the Messiah who has come to provide a way back to the Father and His kingdom. We discussed salvation and how it works. All three of the Trinity participated in salvation, but the Son was fully on display. He became sin for us that we may be considered righteous. We talked about the church that Jesus built, along with the apostles. The church is not perfect because sinful people are a part of it. But still, it is Jesus' body and, therefore, should be respected and not forsaken by the believer.

The sum total of all these teachings leads us to something. We will discuss that. But first, if you are a disciple of Christ, your life is not your own. 1 Corinthians 6:19-20 says, "Don't you realize that your body is the temple of the Holy Spirit, who lives in you and was given to you by God? **You do not belong to yourself**, for God bought you with a **high price**. So you must honor God with your body." When Jesus died for your sins and came back to life on the third day, He bought the rights to your life! Remember this. To call Jesus the Lord of your life, is to say that He owns you. The purpose of your life on the planet earth is not merely to bask in the glory of salvation, waiting to die so you can go to heaven. There is work to be done.

Paul the apostle knew this concept very well. He said in Acts 20:24, "But my life is worth nothing to me unless I use it for finishing the work assigned me by the Lord Jesus—the work of telling others the Good News about the wonderful grace of God." It is best to understand this passage in its context. From Acts 18:23 to 21:17, Paul is on his third missionary journey. There were many hardships during his first two mission trips, also many miracles with scores of people repenting of their sins and turning to Christ. Nearing the end of his journey he feels the Holy Spirit leading him back to Jerusalem. He plans on being obedient, even though the Spirit has also informed him imprisonment and suffering lie ahead. Why would Paul head to Jerusalem even though he knows what will happen? This is why Paul said his life is worthless unless he is working for the Lord which, for anyone, includes spreading the Good News of the kingdom of God.

A Disciples Call:

Matthew 28:18-20 is a passage of scripture where Jesus is speaking to the disciples after His resurrection from the dead. Jesus' statement here is widely known as "The Great Commission." He commands His disciples to do some work while He is gone, until He returns. Jesus said "I have been given all authority in heaven and on earth. Therefore, go and make disciples of all the nations, baptizing them in the name of the Father and the Son and the Holy Spirit. Teach these new disciples to obey all the commands I have given you. And be sure of this: I am with you always, even to the end of the age."

Jesus says He has all authority, which is a significant statement when you consider that many witnessed Him dying on the cross a few days ago. That means He is alive and well, and the mission that He started can continue. "Therefore" go and do the work that I have commanded you to do. But you might be saying: "He commanded His disciples. Not me!" Maybe you only consider yourself to be a Christian and not a disciple. The term "Christian" means "belonging to Christ." That sounds good but let it be noted neither Jesus, the apostles, nor any followers of Jesus coined that term. The word came from outside of the church and was meant to be disrespectful. The first century church used other names to describe themselves like disciples, saints, and brothers. The disciples were first called Christians in Antioch (Acts 11:26). The word was only used two more times in scripture (Acts 26:28, 1 Peter 4:16): once by someone who was considering having faith in Jesus, and by Paul who seems to be telling the listeners to embrace the term by glorifying God with that title.

A disciple accepts and assists in spreading the teachings of another. For instance, the Pharisees once scoffed at a witness of Christ's miracles and claimed to be disciples of Moses (John 9:28). Therefore, a disciple of Jesus accepts and assists in spreading the gospel or teachings of Jesus. The original Greek word for disciple is *mathetes*, which means more than a student. A better definition is "follower" (Matthew 4:19). The fishermen that Jesus called were later called His disciples along with anyone else who cared to follow. They were people who were totally committed to Christ and His teachings.

student. A better definition is "follower" (Matthew 4:19). The fishermen that Jesus called were later called His disciples along with anyone else who cared to follow. They were people who were totally committed to Christ and His teachings.

Some disciples did not stick around very long, though (John 6:66). Jesus was very open about the cost of following Him. He said one must give up everything to follow Him (Luke 14:33). One could not be selfish, either (Matthew 16:24). Also, one was expected to take up their cross (figuratively) just as Christ did (literally). In other words, one was expected to suffer, or die to themselves (Romans 8:13, 17) for Christ just like He suffered and died on the cross.

Let it be noted that a cross was not used for jewelry or tattoos in the first century. That is because it was a means of capital punishment where people were brutally killed during a public display. The church did not even use the cross as a religious symbol until after Constantine abolished punishment by crucifixion in the 4th century. Then the cross was promoted to a Christian symbol. However, the first century church focused more on the resurrection as opposed to the death of Christ.

The cross, as a means of capital punishment, is outdated. So, when we read about Jesus telling His disciples to take up their cross, most if not all of its meaning is lost. If Jesus were walking around the earth bodily today, I suppose He would tell people to carry their electric chair or lethal injection needles! Get the point? In other words, Jesus wants us to know that losing our life and being His disciple go hand in hand. To put it another way, one must lose their identity and replace it with Christ's identity if they want to be Christ's disciple.

Jesus explains all of this very well in Luke 14. For greater clarity, read the entire chapter. But I will specifically discuss verse 25-35. Jesus speaks to a large crowd. His motives might have been to separate the committed people from the tag-a-longs. Jesus is very clear when He states three criteria for being His disciple. First, one must hate their immediate family, including their self, when placed in comparison with Christ. In other words, one must always choose Christ over their family. That is to say, one must love their family less than they love Christ. Second, one must carry their own cross. That is, one must die for the cause of Christ; mainly speaking figuratively, but also referring to a literal death if need be. The 12 original apostles were all martyred except for John (according to many reports and legends). Third, one must give up everything that they own. All that means is, one must see Jesus as Lord or Owner over everything they have or ever will have, including their life.

Jesus understood the gravity of His statements. That is why He told everyone they must "count the cost" of following Him before they sign up to be His disciple. Jesus reasoned with the crowd to prove that counting the costs before making major commitments are a part of everyday life. Jesus wants the people to understand what they are getting into before choosing to call Him Lord.

Christian vs Disciple:

Are you a Christian? If so then that means you, by definition, belong to Christ. If you belong to Christ then that means you have accepted Jesus as your Lord. Anyone belonging to another has relinquished ownership of themselves. Furthermore, if the Lord owns you then you are compelled to do as the Master requests. This is the whole point: the Master commands those who follow Him to lose their life's passions, pleasures, and purpose in order to find and live by the Lord's passions, pleasures, and purpose.

A true Christian is a disciple of Christ. That means they have placed their faith in Jesus Christ, have been born again by the Holy Spirit, and are becoming more and more like Christ every day. A true Christian loves Christ and is an obedient disciple. A true Christian has taken up their cross just as Paul explained when he said in Galatians 2:20, "My old self has been crucified with Christ. It is no longer I who live, but Christ lives in me." A true Christian has counted the cost of following Jesus. They know that the short comings of such a commitment are not even worthy to be compared to the abundant free gifts that are lavished upon them.

Any self-professed believer in Jesus Christ, who is not a disciple, is a Christian in name only! Those who are a Christian in name only are the tares which will be separated from the wheat (Matthew 13:24-30), the goats that will be separated from the sheep (Matthew 25:31-46), and the ones who will cry, "Lord, Lord," on judgement day yet will hear the Lord say, "I never knew you. Get away from me, you who break God's laws" (Matthew 7:22-23).

The Great Commission:

We have already discussed Matthew 28:18-20, widely known as "The Great Commission." A commission is an instruction, command, or duty given to a group of people. Many see Acts 1:8 as part of the Great Commission as well: "But you will receive power when the Holy Spirit comes upon you. And you will be my witnesses, telling people about me everywhere—in Jerusalem, throughout Judea, in Samaria, and to the ends of the earth." The Great Commission is empowered by the Holy Spirit so Christ's disciples can be His witnesses in our cities, states, countries, and beyond. The word "witness," as used in the above scripture, is not a religious term. One may think of a witness for Christ just as a witness is used in a court of law. A witness has observed something for themselves and have been employed by the court to speak about their observations. The best witnesses do not speak on hearsay or opinion. They only discuss their personal observations concerning a particular person(s) or event. That is what a disciple for Christ does; that is, discuss with others in their city, state, or country what they have observed. A disciple for Christ as observed who they were before Christ, their salvation in Christ, and their new life due to the Holy Spirit residing in them.

The church was being persecuted in the first century. In 1 Peter chapter 3 Peter speaks about how one should respond concerning this. He said "do not repay evil for evil" (verse 9) and, "the Lord will watch over you if you do right" (verse 12). But even if persecution comes upon you, one should not worry or be afraid" (verse 14). "Instead, worship the Lord and be ready to explain the Christian hope that you have to anyone who asks" (verse 15). What is Peter saying? Even those who are suffering still have an obligation to tell others about the gospel relating to Jesus Christ! One should not hold their life so dear that they forsake the transmission of the word of God.

Paul does a great job of explaining the marks of discipleship in 2 Corinthians 5:17-21. After reading this, we learn that anyone who belongs to Christ is a new person with a new life! God has charged us with the job of reconciling people to Christ by speaking a message of reconciliation. Therefore, we are Christ's ambassadors who are witnesses to Christ's wonderful gift. God is making His case for Christ through us when we tell someone, "Come back to God!"

What is an ambassador? He/she is an accredited diplomat sent by a country as its official representative to a foreign country. What does this have to do with disciples? Remember that disciples are those who are saved by Christ and have been given citizenship into the kingdom of God due to Christ's precious gift and their professed allegiance to Him. Because of our new citizenship, we should see ourselves as foreigners, sojourners, aliens, strangers, or exiles to the current countries that we reside (1 Peter 2:11). In contrast, the Gentiles were told that they were no longer foreigners or strangers to the kingdom of God since they now had been given the Holy Spirit (Ephesians 2:18-19). Therefore, when we tell someone about the gospel, as illustrated in the Bible, it is like we are standing on foreign soil representing another country or government, just as one of the United States ambassadors does when he/she is in France, Canada, or some other nation. Disciples are to represent Jesus Christ in an official capacity in foreign nations or communities. They are charged with promoting Christ's interests, both locally and abroad. Let it be known that the kingdom of God is the only nation that will stand for eternity and anyone who wishes to have eternal life must choose between God and country and profess allegiance to Jesus Christ.

Ushering in His Kingdom:

Disciples should want to spread the gospel for unselfish reasons. We do not want to hoard salvation for ourselves, we want to share it with the world. However, there is a lingering motivating factor that should lead all followers of Christ to prepare and organize for active service. God's kingdom is already on the earth on an invisible level but the active service of the saints will usher in His kingdom on a more tangible scale.

In Matthew chapter 24, Jesus is prophesying about the final days of the world. Read the entire chapter for greater understanding. Jesus said buildings will fall to the ground, false messiahs will reveal themselves, wars will break out, and there will be natural disasters. He said God's people will be persecuted, many will fall away from the faith, false prophets will deceive, and sin will be all over the world. Yet, during all of this, a major activity will be taking place. "And the Good News about the Kingdom will be preached throughout the whole world, so that all nations will hear it; **and then the end will come**" (verse14). The "end" that Jesus speaks of is His return to earth or, as many refer to it, His "Second Coming." Jesus then describes His return and what signs will proceed it. The greatest sign is the gospel being preached everywhere.

All disciples should take part in the transmission of the gospel. Even right this moment, the kingdom of God is "forcefully advancing" (Matthew 11:12) throughout the world and there is plenty of work to do! Jesus said "The harvest is great, but the workers are few. So pray to the Lord who is in charge of the harvest; ask him to send more workers into his fields." (Luke 10:2).

There are many ways to participate in the Great Commission of Jesus Christ but there are probably three main ways. First, we all need to pray. Prayer is necessary so more workers can enter the field, the Holy Spirit can convict people of their sin, Christian leaders can be beyond reproach, the true gospel of the kingdom of God can be preached throughout the world, the down trodden can be served, and so much more. Second, we all need to give. There are two facets to this. There is giving financially, which is necessary to fund the mission in many areas, and there is giving of ourselves in personal service to our communities. We all must give back to God. We do this by giving to people or organizations in Jesus' name. We also need to give of ourselves in service. Jesus said that if one wants to be the greatest or a leader in His kingdom then they must also be a servant in His kingdom (Matthew 20:26-27).

The last way to get involved in the Great Commission is to be a witness for Christ. You cannot be ashamed of Jesus Christ. Jesus said, "If anyone is ashamed of me and my message, the Son of Man will be ashamed of that person when he returns in his glory and in the glory of the Father and the holy angels" (Luke 9:26). That is why Paul exclaimed, "For I am not ashamed of this Good News about Christ. It is the power of God at work, saving everyone who believes—the Jew first and also the Gentile." (Romans 1:16). It does not make any sense to receive such a precious gift from the Lord and then hide it away just as the wicked servant did in Jesus' parable in Matthew 25:14-30. All those who have been saved by Christ are the "light of the world" and no one lights a lamp just to hide it. "Instead, a lamp is placed on a stand, where it gives light to everyone in the house" (Matthew 5:15).

You may feel like you are inadequate and have nothing to say or add to the Great Commission but, as we learn from a great story about a blind man in John chapter 9, it's about what He's done for us individually, that can impact others around us so greatly. Read the chapter for yourself but Jesus heals a blind man, and the man tried to tell others what had happened but many did not believe him. He was interrogated by the people as they waged an investigation. The man was asked many questions about who Jesus was, but he did not have any information to satisfy their examination because he never knew Jesus before he was healed. The people took the man to the Pharisees who then cross-examined the formerly blind man, hoping to find information they could arrest Jesus with and convict Him. The Pharisees did not want to believe that Jesus had performed a miracle. They even questioned the man's parents as to whether he had ever been blind before. Finally, the Pharisees questioned the man one more time, trying get him to testify that Jesus was a sinner but the formerly blind man did not have any more information in which to answer the barrage of questions. Finally fed up, he answered intently, "I don't know whether he is a sinner," the man replied. "But I know this: I was blind, and now I can see!" (Verse 25).

Being a witness for Christ does not mean you need to go to Bible school, become a preacher, or be in the public eye. You just need to tell people what you know. That's it! Just like the blind man, who had less information than you do right now, you can let the light of Christ shine through you and change the world! You are empowered by the Holy Spirit who will give you the wisdom of what to say when the time comes.

Exponential Growth:

We previously discussed how the church grew exponentially in the past. The most notable examples are that of the first century church and the underground church in China. Exponential growth is growth that increases by a steady measure. There has been a decline in growth rate over the last 200 years during the Scientific Revolution. The church, or the kingdom of God, still has the ability to grow at a very high rate. It must get back to that again if we are to see our good Lord return in power and glory. The work of Jesus' commission to His disciples will be at the forefront of this miracle.

How fast is exponential growth? Let's find out as we consider this riddle: A father complained that his son's allowance of $5 per week was too much. So the son came up with a solution. He told his dad to pay a penny for the first day of the month, 2 cents for the second, 4 cents for the third, 8 cents for the fourth, and so on for everyday of the month. The boy's father agreed to the deal. Who was more clever, the father or son? If you answered the son, you are correct! That is because the son's allowance on the 31st day of the month would total

$10,737,418.24. Now that is exponential growth! You might not believe this riddle could happen but do the math for yourself. If you showed it all on a graph then there would be small incremental grow until day 26. Then the graph line would shoot straight up, increasing "exponentially." This proves that a very small amount, which is constantly doubled every day, can turn into an unbelievably large number in a very short amount of time.

Exponential growth can also be seen on your loan payments. The original payoff amount increases steadily over time. This is due to something called compound interest. Basically, it is interest on interest. A percentage of interest, based on the principle or original amount, is generated, then that sum is added back to the principle. This increases the amount of interest generated for the next period, then that amount is added back to the principle. This goes on and on for the life of the loan. The longer the loan lives, the faster and faster the interest grows.

Kingdom Advancement:

The potential for great kingdom growth can also be understood by examining the spread of viruses. Viruses spread from person to person. One person can effect hundreds of people. This is by the droplets that fly out when someone coughs or sneezes. The tiny drops move through the air and land on the mouths and noses of people, and on surfaces that are often touched by others. Therefore, one person can turn into tens overnight, hundreds in days, and thousands in weeks. Each person that is affected becomes someone who can infect others. So, it is easy to see how the flu advances so quickly year after year, resulting in the closing of schools and businesses.

There is another example to consider: multi-level marketing. Made famous by Amway, it is a way for a company to sell its products by recruiting people who sell the product for them to the general public. Then those people recruit other people to do the same thing. The basic model for this type of business is this: 1 person finds 6 people to commit to the business, then each of those 6 people find 6 people of their own to commit to the business. Each person who signs up is under the original 1st person who is at the top of the tree. However, each person starts their own tree as soon as they bring people in. Therefore, the original first person went from 1 person to 36 people, each one generating income of their own which the 1st person gets some sort of commission for. This is the business model shown to many people each year to demonstrate how easily it can be done.

"Each one teach one" is a saying people use to show how easy it is for everyone to get involved in a particular activity. However, the kingdom of God is supposed to advance faster than that. Peter preached the first church sermon ever and that resulted in 3000 people coming into faith in Christ. I know that will not happen every time but it is clearly possible. You might be saying, "But that was a different time and place!" That is true. But we still have the Holy Spirit who engineers these movements and makes them possible at any time and place. We know how bad things are getting on this planet anytime we watch the news. So, the church growing exponentially seems very impossible. That is not true! Ordinary people cannot make this happen. This has always been the case, though. Jesus was telling His disciples that it is easier for a camel to go through the eye of a needle than for some people to repent and turn to Him. The disciples were astonished at Jesus' statement and wondered out loud if anyone in the world could be saved. Jesus responded, "Humanly speaking, it is impossible. But with God everything is possible." (Matthew 19:16-26).

THE CONCLUSION: DISCOVERING YOUR PURPOSE

We love inventions. That is because they make our lives easier. What would we do without the vacuum cleaner? Do you want to live without air conditioning? What about the microwave or the calculator? Let's not forget the internet! By the way, the first general purpose computer was invented in 1946. It weighed 30 tons! Lights dimmed in sections of Philadelphia when it was turned on for the first time. Despite its size, it could only perform one task at a time. The smart phones we keep in our pockets are more powerful than that! The list goes on and on.

Who invented any of those things? Who invented the radio? Most people do not know the inventor of anything they use on a daily basis. Why is that? It is because we love the invention but not the inventor. In actuality, the inventor should be celebrated. After all, the invention was invisible until it was made tangible. That is because ideas are invisible. Therefore, when you hold a hair brush in your hand, you are holding someone's idea. Thankfully, Samuel Firey made his idea public in 1870 which made it possible for Lyda Newman to improve upon his brush idea in 1898.

Before an inventor can take their product to market, they must let everyone know what the product can be used for, how it works, and how to maintain it. Otherwise they are the only one that knows the purpose of the product. So I suggest you read the instructions before you assemble or use anything for the first time.

The inventor knows the product inside and out, and must give you information to bring you up to speed. I got an electric shaver for Christmas that is specifically designed for the head. It can be used for the face, technically. However, I found that it is too big for comfort. It is a wet/dry electric shaver which means it can be used in the shower and/or with shaving cream or gel. The directions warn against using shaving oil because it will ruin the shaver. That is information that I needed to know. I can still use shaving oil if I want to but that is misuse and abuse. That is why the company would void my warranty. Using something outside of the constraints of its designer is dangerous. Always remember this: Purpose is always found in the mind of the maker!

Adam and Eve:

Mankind was made in the image of his maker, God the Creator. God informed Adam of his purpose when he said, "Be fruitful and multiply" (Genesis 1:28). Man was given everything! If he had only been given one thing then he would have cherished it. But he focused on the one thing that he could not have: the tree of the knowledge of good and evil. God warned Adam that he was not designed to eat from that tree and would die in the process. Adam ignored the instructions. Adam and Eve thought that they knew themselves and creation better than the One who invented the universe. Big mistake! Consequentially, creation was ruined.

Adam and Eve misunderstood their potential. Potent means power. So potential is the power to become something or someone. Potential comes from the Maker. God thought of Adam, set a limit for his potential, and then created him from the dirt. Satan tricked Adam and Eve into believing that God was holding out or lying to them about what they could become. They took the bait which voided the agreement they had with God and were cast away.

Adam and Eve began to view themselves incorrectly. They saw their nakedness as shameful and Eve began to desire to rule over her husband. They tried to fix the problem with leaves but only their Maker could find a solution. The animal skins represented an innocent animal which foreshadowed the ultimate solution in Jesus Christ.

Mankind has been looking for his purpose or potential ever since. We try to find our purpose in all sorts of things. Most of them are counterfeit. Just like Adam and Eve, we are tricked into believing we are less than what God envisioned when He purposed us in His thoughts. You may not see yourself as worth very much or capable of great things but that is a lie! Perhaps you have found what you define as success. However, without God's purpose, your success is not as powerful as it could be.

The Original Tri-Unity of Man:

Mankind was designed to be a triune being. This would consist of the spirit, soul, and body. Remember, God made man in His image. God is triune consisting of the Father, Son, and Holy Spirit. These three distinct persons of God are in perfect unity. Man consists of spirit, soul, and body; however, they are not in unity with each other. That is because the spirit has the conscience to do right while negotiating the soul's will to do what feels good. Upon salvation, the Holy Spirit ensures a more informed conscience in which to judge the intents of the soul and actions of the body.

Man is an invisible spirit who owns a soul and lives in a body chamber. The spirit/soul is who man is without a body. This spirit and soul are connected. The spirit (man) is immediately restored by the Holy Spirit upon salvation during justification. His soul must be restored over time in a process called sanctification. The body is not much more than a shell which gives man the legal license to live in a physical natural setting. The soul has three parts: the mind, will, and emotions (all within a spirit). These three parts equal a man's intelligence.

The Holy Spirit's job is to tell the soul of man exactly what God is thinking. Then the soul takes this intelligence and relays it to the body. The spirit (man) needs to be completely connected to God in order to receive the correct information for the soul. This can all happen in reverse as well. Here is a real example. My eyes or body saw a friend of mine living a lifestyle that I thought I should be living. My soul (mind, will, emotions) took that information for the spirit to judge. The spirit (which was saved and in communion with the Holy Spirit) told my soul that was incorrect information. Actually, the spirit told me "The first will be the last, and the last will be the first" (Matthew 20:16). Therefore, my soul relayed that to my body. That was a major lesson in my life which is to not believe everything the eyes see.

Let's go back to the Garden of Eden. The tree of the knowledge of good and evil was forbidden. But what is so bad or wrong about knowledge? Man was only supposed to know what God wanted him to know. Man was not designed to deal with the knowledge of the relationship between good and evil. Adam and Eve did not understand this, but they didn't have to.

All they had to do was believe that they already had enough information for the situation. That information was to not eat of the tree.

They saw something that seemed to be good. That information went to their soul or mind, will, and emotions. They ignored the information they had already been given by the spirit which was in communion with God. The original use of the spirit was to connect man with ALL necessary information needed for life via the Spirit of God. The soul would use this information to tell the body to function accordingly (obedience).

Everything changed when Adam and Eve ate of the tree. The action made it possible for mankind's spirit/soul to see the information the body gives as more highly regarded than the information that the Holy Spirit gives. Now the majority of mankind gleans information from the universe using the five senses of the body (sight, hearing, smell, taste, and touch) and judging it based on their intellect (soul) while their conscience (spirit) is largely inactive. However, men/women of God take in information from the body and give it to God so He can tell them what to conclude from it. That is why archeologists who are Christian find information and conclude differently than archeologists who are not Christian.

God's Plan:

God has a specific plan for your life that no one else has been given. His plan for you includes a purpose or reason for you being born and a level of potential for you to exhaust. It does not matter what your five senses tell you or what other people tell you. You have been designed for greatness! Just because you have not fulfilled your potential yet does not mean you have ran out of it.

You may look at other people who are winning and succeeding and think that they are better than you are. That is not true! In fact, all mankind are made out of the same stuff: dirt (Genesis 2:7). So if other people can succeed, so can you. All you have to do is discover your purpose so you can maximize your potential in life.

There are several ways to discover what your purpose for life is. You just need to take inventory of yourself. Where do you like to go? What do you like to do? What are some of your strengths and talents? What are your desires? Whatever makes you angry or frustrated may be something you are meant to correct or fix.

I will use me as an example. Many people used to say that I should be a lawyer. They would say that I liked to argue. They must have also believed that I was good at it. I certainly did love how lawyers were portrayed on television and movies. A real life lawyer told me that the profession is nothing like that. He told me that it is a lot of reading and studying. Court appearances are not what most lawyers do on a regular basis. Overall, law is not that glamourous. It is sitting at your desk and performing average lawyer tasks. That did not sound interesting to me.

Fast forward many years later. I discovered that the gifts people saw in me that lead them to believe I should be a lawyer, were actually gifts God wanted to use in me to argue and explain the things of God. As I did that more and more, I realized that I also had a gift for teaching. It would have been great to know all of that when I was in my teens and twenties.

You may not discover what your purpose and potential level is right away. But answer the questions above and pray about it. Don't stop praying until you get an answer. You may not get your answer all at once. It is very likely that it will come in bits and pieces over time. Just keep praying and keep pressing! You must find out what your purpose is so that you can maximize your potential. Do not be satisfied with your current life. Even if you have found success and gained riches, that may or may not be related to the purpose God has for you. Remember that you cannot set your own purpose in life. Only the Maker can set the purpose for that which He makes.

Your body may be taking in information regarding all of the obstacles that are blocking you from fulfilling your purpose and potential. But all you need is God the Creator on your side. The Lord has supplied you with limitless resources from heaven which are at your disposal. These resources can be invisible like wisdom or favor. There are also visible resources like money, help from others, or materials. All God has to do is reallocate His assets (which includes everything in existence) to you on demand. Your job is to pray and have faith.

Part of God's plan is to give you whatever you need to succeed. The Lord is going to send you a mentor to train you in your next venture. Maybe God will give you a burden to go back to school but then will give you the means to pay for it. Others around you will succeed but they will only get what their efforts and talents can produce. You will have success that is based on what the Lord can do, not what you can do alone. You may have to work harder than you ever have before. Your victory will be congruent to God's abilities and not your own.

God will cause you to win because He wants His plan to work. Just make sure you are not giving God your designed plans and then telling Him to bless them. You must receive His plans for your life which are already blessed. Many people have misunderstood Psalm 37:4: "Take delight in the LORD, and he will give you your heart's desires." Some think that God will give you whatever you want. That is not true. The scripture means that if a person delights in the Lord then God will implant desires in them. These will be desires that God wants them to have and pursue. When you are pursuing desires and goals that God has caused you to have then, you and God are on the same page, so to speak.

The Potential of a Seed:

I throw away the core anytime that I finish eating an apple. I don't have any need for it but that does not mean that it is useless. Every apple core holds seeds that have far reaching potential. Every apple seed holds the potential for an apple orchard. How? It is because every seed holds the potential to grow a tree that produces apples that drop seeds that grow trees that produce apples that drop seeds…and so on. So the potential of a seed far exceeds the initial tree that comes from it.

This is clearly stated in the Bible as God makes a promise to Abram: "I will make you into a great nation" (Genesis 12:2). Abram had great potential. He was just one man, he housed a great nation. God assigned this potential to him. Abram would not have been able to produce such a great nation on his own but it was made possible with God. Abram could have started a chain of human reproduction without God but the nation he was promised to be the father of was to become a very special nation. That is why God told Abram "All the families on earth will be blessed through you" (Genesis 12:3). All the families on earth? Wow! That is a load of potential. God saw it to completion.

The power of the seed to become what it was meant to be has been placed on the inside of it. Although an apple seed seems inadequate, it holds an apple forest on the inside. In comparison, a great nation was on the inside of Abram. Likewise, your ultimate potential has already been placed on the inside of you. It will take God to bring it out.

You have to stop being what you want to be and start being what God wants you to be. You have to die to yourself so that Christ can live in you (Galatians 2:20). Any natural seed has to do the same thing. Jesus once said, "I tell you the truth, unless a kernel of wheat is planted in the soil and dies, it remains alone. But its death will produce many new kernels—a plentiful harvest of new lives" (John 12:24). When you look in the mirror, you may see yourself as small and irrelevant. But it is what's on the inside of you that matters.

Seed to Harvest:

Jesus understood the power of a seed. That is why He compared it to His word. We must remember that God used His words to create the universe. Think about that for a minute! God created something out of nothing by speaking. The Bible says that the earth was formless, empty, and dark (Genesis 1). Basically, the earth did not exist or was invisible without natural attributes. But God assigned potential to an empty space. Then He said "Let there be light." I think it probably sounded like this: BOOM! All of a sudden, the ideas and expression of God, which were invisible, could now be seen.

The parable of the seed and the sower can be read in Matthew 13. Jesus talks about a seed and four different soils. The seed represents the message of the kingdom or God's word. The soils represent particular types of people. The first set of people hear the message but do not understand. The next group hear the message and receive it at first. But they quit as soon as problems arise. Another group hears the message and receives it initially. But, sadly, the worries and cares of everyday life are seen as most important. Therefore, the message is not able to produce any fruit in them. The final group heard the message and understood it. That allowed them to produce a harvest of 30, 60, or 100 times more than the original seed.

The Lord will reveal to you what your purpose is on the earth. You just have to pray and wait on the Lord to reveal the secret to you. The answer may come all at once or steadily over a period of time. Once the revelation is given, it will be God's word on the inside of you. The Holy Spirit will dictate to you exactly what God wants you to know about yourself. Knowing your purpose will produce a passion within you. This purpose and passion is invisible. Just like the earth in Genesis 1, your purpose and passion will have no form or natural qualities to it but they will have potential. When you are able to become like the last group of people mentioned in the parable, the invisible purpose, passion, and potential inside of you will be brought to light.

There are two different realms at work here. A realm is like a domain of activity. One realm is the spirit or invisible realm. The other is the natural or visible realm. The spirit realm has constant activity going on that we cannot perceive with our natural senses. We cannot see God, angels, or the demonic principalities at work around us (Ephesians 6:12). The natural realm is everything around us that we can sense with our bodies. Even the wind is natural. We cannot see it but we can feel it.

God's word of purpose to you will be invisible. It will be like a seed that is hidden in the ground. God's word will be hidden on the inside of you. Don't be like the people who don't take time to understand it. Don't be like the ones who allow problems and worries to take the place of God's word in their life. If you can take God's word of purpose for you and hold on to it for long enough, it will produce a harvest that can be seen! Your purpose, passion, and potential will move from the "I can't see it" realm to the, "there it is, I can see it" realm!

God's purpose on the inside of you will exist without form. It is your job to have faith. That is because faith is the assurance about things we cannot see (Hebrews 11:1). Then God will bring a harvest out of you that people can see. It is important to note that human potential without Godly purpose will bring destruction. You must do things God's way. Wait for things to happen in His timing. Pray. This is how the people of God get things done.

God Must Get the Glory:

God will never lead you to complete a task that you can execute on your own. This is a very important principle. God wants to get glory for Himself. Not you. For God to get the glory, it has to be obvious that He is doing the work. Then, when the work is done, He can receive the fame that comes along with it.

Review the story in the book of Exodus: chapters 1-14. God tells Moses that He wants to free the Israelites. Moses is told to tell Pharaoh to let the people go. God chose to harden Pharaoh's heart. In other words, God made him stubborn. God did not want Pharaoh to let the people go easily. Why? Because if he let them go easily then the world would have said, "Pharaoh is so gracious! What a benevolent leader!" God wanted to be made famous from all of this. He wanted to have the glory, not Moses or Pharaoh. So God inflicted 10 calamities upon Egypt in order to force Pharaoh to let the people go. Because of this, even the Egyptians knew that it was the God of the Israelites that was doing this to them. Even today we can read this story of miracles and have our faith increase by knowing that God can do anything, including defy nature.

The point is that, in order for God to get the glory, He has to do the work. But, there is no need for Him to do the work if you or I can do it all by our self. Do you understand? God told Moses to do a job but he felt inadequate due to his speech impediment. So God gave him a speaker, Aaron. Then, Moses could not convince Pharaoh to let the people go. So God sent the calamities, including the parting of the Red Sea. In other words, God called Moses, all the while knowing that he would be unable to complete the task on his own. Ultimately, God would have to do it himself.

This is the way God works. He chooses to use foolish, powerless, despised, and worthless things to defeat the wise, powerful, and important things of this world (1 Corinthians 1:27). He does it this way to make sure that He gets the glory from the success. Read the story of the battle of Jericho (Joshua 6) or the story of Gideon (Judges 6-7). Both stories prove this principle.

The Secret to Success:

God has purpose for you. When your purpose has been fulfilled, there will no longer be a reason for you to live on the earth. That will be the end of the race for you (2 Timothy 4:7). It will be time for you to go to heaven. Then your maker will tell you, "Well done!" (Matthew 25:23). But, until then, there is work to do. If you do things the Lord's way then your success (that is really God's success) is inevitable.

There is a secret to success. Many self-help books have been written on this subject. The information they give is pretty good most of the time. Basically, you get out of life what you put into it. But this is not a self-help book. This is a God-help-me book! It is designed to help you harness the power of God so you can get out of life what He has put into it.

The entire message of God is about this secret. Some don't know anything about it. Some know but don't understand it. Others understand it but don't have any faith in it. "And this is the secret: Christ lives in you" (Colossians 1:27). If you have repented of your sins and have professed allegiance to Jesus then the Holy Spirit (Jesus' spirit) lives in you. That means God's wisdom, power, and strength is in you too. You can have the wisdom of God, perform miracles, and endure the stresses of life all because Christ is in you. This is how you will find success. God's plan for your life will work because He is on the inside of you making it work! All you have to do is have faith and yield to the Holy Spirit.

Do you think you are not wise? Use God's wisdom (Proverbs 3:5-6). Do you not have enough money to complete the assignment? Use God's resources (Philippians 4:19). Do you not have enough faith? God will increase it (Mark 9:24). Is God calling you to an arena where success is close to impossible? Other people's success has nothing to do with yours (Psalm 91:7). What other excuses do you have that is stopping you from fulfilling God's purpose for your life? This is what God is saying to you right now: "My grace is all you need. My power works best in weakness" (2 Corinthians 12:9). If you are weak, inadequate, or unable, God works best in you too!

A Few Guidelines:

You will never truly know your purpose in this life until you accept Jesus as your Lord and Savior. Only the Maker knows exactly what He designed you for. Therefore, you need an open line of communication with Him to discover what it is. Jesus will do that for you (John 14:6). God can speak to you directly or indirectly through another person but the word will be coming from Him.

Only disciples will maximize their potential. It is one thing to know your purpose but it is quite another to get all you can out of it. Disciples obey Christ and follow Him where ever He leads them. God knows the best way to maximize your potential. Therefore, you must take heed when He speaks and move as directed.

Purpose is only designed by God to benefit mankind. Remember that while you are searching for yours. I used to think my purpose in life was to be rich and have material possessions. But that is impossible! There isn't anything wrong with having money and things. However, that is not an example of purpose. For instance, maybe someone thinks that their purpose is to be an NFL linebacker but the only benefit it provides is entertainment, which is short lived.

Entertainment is simply a temporary escape from the stresses of life. However, God may want someone to be an NFL linebacker so He can use the earthly status it provides to bring about change in people or society. Jesse Owens is a great example of this. He was an American Olympic athlete who won four gold medals in the 1936 Berlin Games. He is best known for defying Hitler's attempt to prove the theory of Aryan racial superiority. The people of Berlin saw Jesse, who was an African American, as a hero.

Do you desire to be the strongest man alive? That's okay, I guess but it is not a purpose from God unless He wants to use it to benefit mankind in some way. Do you understand? God can give you purpose in anything, but it will always be for the cause of service to your fellow man.

You may be thinking that there are a lot of people out there who are reaching their purpose and potential without faith in God or Jesus. It may seem that way but remember that people like that are only accomplishing in life what their intellect and physical capabilities will allow them to. Their achievements may surpass most by comparison, but God could have done much more with them. Furthermore, the decisions, accomplishments, and overall power of God will be felt throughout eternity. All of mankind's successes are short lived. One day this version of the earth will not exist anymore and all of man's accomplishments will go away with it. God wants to do something in you that is greater than you or anyone else could ever envision. 1 Corinthians 2:9 says it best: "No eye has seen, no ear has heard, and no mind has imagined what God has prepared for those who love him."

Mask Off:

Let us consider a hypothetical situation. Imagine you have just graduated from college with honors. A life of success is ahead of you, right? But the only job that you can get hired for is a dishwasher at minimum wage. Then you keep putting out applications but no one is hiring. How would you feel about that? Would you be excited about going to work every day? Would you give 100% effort even though you are over educated and over qualified for the job? If 5 years goes by and you are still a dishwasher, would you be depressed as you pay back student loans that seemed to promise you a better life? Would you be proud to tell your friends and family that you are a dishwasher?

Now let us consider the same scenario except that your father is CEO of the company that you wash dishes for. Your father made a deal with you that, if you paid your dues at the lowest level of the company while keeping a great attitude and work ethic, a multi-million dollar position would be waiting for you when the time is right. How would you feel about the dishwashing position then?

If you had the right mindset then you would be able to deal with dishwashing in a healthy way. Why? Because you would know that, deep down, you are not a dishwasher. You are a multi-million dollar heir temporarily working as a dish-washer! You would know how great you are on the inside even if no one else had any idea.

This is how most of us live our lives. Except that we have no idea that we are heirs of God's glory (Romans 8:17). So we accept whatever rut that we are in. God has a plan and purpose for your life but you have to know who you are first. That way you will know where you are headed.

Take your mask off! Stop pretending! Wipe that grin off your face while you fake like your life is going the way it should. Stop chasing the Joneses and comparing yourself to other people. Stop acting like the family business makes you happy when it really doesn't. Stop saying that you have peaked in life. Stop ignoring your dreams. You are greater than you know. Be who you are supposed to be!

You are who God says you are. Gideon called himself the least in his family but God called him a mighty hero (Judges 6). Moses wanted to focus on his speech impediment instead of God's power. So the Lord asked him this: "Who makes a person's mouth? Who decides whether people speak or do not speak...?" (Exodus 4). Jesse showed Samuel seven of his best sons but Samuel was instructed by the Lord not to judge on appearance for the Lord looks at the heart. Then the least son, David, comes out from the field and is anointed king (1 Samuel 16). The rich young ruler was wealthy and wanted to stay that way. However Jesus had other plans for him (Luke 18). Peter was an eager disciple who was always ready to fight but he cowardly denied Jesus three times in the courtyard. In shame, he ran away to his old life as a fisherman. Jesus found him on the seashore and reminded him of his purpose (John 18; 21). Peter ended up preaching the first sermon in church history (Acts 2). Paul murdered Christians for a living. That is until Jesus got a hold of him on the road to Damascus (Acts 9). He ended up writing close to 30% of the New Testament.

Take your mask off! Let the Lord bring the real you out for everyone to see. Stop hiding behind smiles and polite conversation. Humble yourself and do things God's way. Pray for direction. Seek after the heart of God. Repent for going your own way. The Lord will show you His plan. Then live your life…without the mask.

REFERENCES

Bevere, John. Killing Kryptonite: Destroy What Kills Your Strength. Palmer Lake. Colorado. Messenger International, 2017.

Wikipedia. "Chalcedonian Creed." https://simple.wikipedia.org/wiki/Chalcedonian_Creed (accessed October 18, 2019).

Gudem, Wayne. Bible Doctrine: Essential Teachings of the Christian Faith. Grand Rapids, Michigan. Zondervan Academic, 1999.

Frangipane, Francis. The Three Battlegrounds. Cedar Rapids, Iowa. Arrow Publications 1977.